Modern Capitalism
and other essays

Paul M. Sweezy

D1603366

New York and London

Contents

Foreword

The essays collected in this volume, written over a period of fifteen years (1956-1971), are divided into two parts. The first part comprises eight essays dealing with various aspects of capitalist reality and criticizing latter-day theories of capitalist reality. The second part brings together three essays expounding and evaluating Marx's contribution to our understanding of capitalism as it has developed in the century since the publication of *Das Kapital*.

There are repetitions in both parts, not only in my own exposition but also in the quotations from the works of others. I should have liked to eliminate these repetitions, but it proved impossible to do so without destroying surrounding contexts. Each essay has its own distinctive purpose and emphases, while at the same time being closely related to one or more of the others in point of subject matter. That there should be a certain amount of overlapping was therefore unavoidable.

There is one issue on which I would like to add a few words to what is said in several of these essays, most particularly "Marx and the Proletariat" beginning on page

147. Viewing capitalism as a global system made up of a few exploiting imperialist countries and many exploited dependent countries, I argue that the primary or principal contradiction of the system in the present period has not been, as Marx clearly believed it to be in his time, between the bourgeoisie and the proletariat in the developed capitalist metropolis, nor yet, as history proved it to be in the period 1870-1945, among the advanced imperialist powers themselves. Rather the primary contradiction in the post-Second World War period has been between the metropolis dominated by the United States and revolutionary national liberation movements in the Third World. This thesis is supported, in my view irrefutably, by certain undeniable facts: there have been no revolutions in the metropolis; conflict among the imperialist powers, while present, has never approached the intensity of earlier periods (1870-1918 and 1933-1945); and the great world-shaking events of the past quarter century have been the triumph of the Chinese Revolution and the defeat of U.S. imperialism in Southeast Asia.

What accounts for this turn of events and for the nonfulfillment of Marx's expectations of successful socialist revolutions in the most advanced capitalist countries? My answer, reduced to its barest essentials, is that technological and structural changes in the advanced capitalist countries have turned what was a revolutionary proletariat at the height of the industrial revolution into a much more variegated and predominantly nonrevolutionary proletariat in the period of developed monopoly capitalism. In the meantime, developments on a world scale have seen the exploited masses in the Third World gradually transformed into a revolutionary force, capable (as China and Vietnam have proved) of challenging and defeating the technologically most advanced capitalist nations.

For holding these views, I have been accused of revisionism, abandoning Marxism, and similar transgressions and delinquencies. Insofar as these accusations are merely an emanation of the dogmatic mind, which is always with us, they interest me very little. But I am sure that in many cases they are a good deal more than that. I think they often reflect a feeling, or perhaps even a conviction, that anyone holding these views must have lost all hope for the working classes of the advanced countries. And since a revolution without, not to say against, the working class is impossible in these countries (a proposition which I fully accept), this would amount to writing off the possibility of revolution in the very regions which Marxists have traditionally assumed to be their natural breeding ground.

I must disagree with this conclusion. The nonrevolutionary character of the United States and the other advanced capitalist countries *today* seems to me so obvious that I cannot see how it can be denied by anyone with an elementary respect for facts. But this does not mean that this is a permanent state of affairs, nor does it mean that revolutionaries should shun or downgrade educational and organizing activity among workers. In "Marx and the Proletariat" I tried to show that the working class has been through revolutionary and nonrevolutionary phases in the past, that it was nonrevolutionary in the period of manufacture and revolutionary in the period of what Marx called modern industry, roughly the first half of the nineteenth century. I also tried to show that this was Marx's view and not my own invention. What I added was an explanation of why the working class became nonrevolutionary again in the period of monopoly capitalism. And what I would now like to add further is my belief that we are presently entering a period in which the working class in the advanced capitalist countries will once again become revolutionary.

To attempt to support this position in any detail would go far beyond the scope of a brief foreword. Suffice it to say that the French events of May 1968 showed in a particularly clear way how rapidly a crisis in class relations in an advanced capitalist country can escalate into what can only be described as a prerevolutionary situation. But it also showed no less clearly that the past hundred years, more or less, of reformism in both economics and politics has allowed a nonrevolutionary structure and leadership to become deeply rooted in the working-class movement. It will take a great deal more than spontaneity and combativeness, both of which the French workers displayed in abundance, to overcome this heritage of reformism, now institutionalized in both trade unions and traditional working-class parties. This will certainly not be quickly or easily achieved, but until it has been achieved it will be mere playing with words to speak of a revolutionary working class. In the meantime, the reason for believing that it can be and will be achieved is, at bottom, the increasingly evident fact that global capitalism is in a deepening crisis from which there is no escape within the framework of the system. Up to now the working classes of the advanced capitalist countries have gotten off relatively easily, but henceforth it is probable to the point of near certainty that the burdens of the system's disintegration will fall ever more heavily on their shoulders. And that will make all the difference.

—Paul M. Sweezy

New York City
April 10, 1972

I
Modern Capitalism

Modern Capitalism

I

I want to begin with a fairly lengthy passage from Joseph A. Schumpeter's *History of Economic Analysis:*[1] *

> What distinguishes the "scientific" economist from all the other people who think, talk, and write about economic topics is a command of techniques that we class under three heads: history, statistics, and "theory." The three together make up what we shall call economic analysis.
>
> Of these fundamental fields, economic history—which issues into and includes present-day facts—is by far the most important. I wish to state right now that if, starting my work in economics afresh, I were told that I could study only one of these three but could have my choice, it would be economic history that I should choose. And this on three grounds. First, the subject matter of

This essay appeared in the June 1971 issue of *Monthly Review*. It is based on an article written for a Japanese encyclopedia, and with the addition of part I as an introduction, it has been presented in somewhat modified form to several university audiences.

*All references appear at the end of the chapter.

economics is essentially a unique process in historic time. Nobody can hope to understand the economic phenomena of any, including the present, epoch who has not an adequate command of historical *facts* and an adequate amount of historical *sense* or of what may be described as *historical experience*. Second, the historical report cannot be purely economic but must inevitably reflect also "institutional" facts that are not purely economic: therefore it affords the best method for understanding how economic and non-economic facts *are* related to one another and how the various social sciences should be related to one another. [Elsewhere in *History* Schumpeter says: Owing to the unreliability of "theories" on this subject, I personally believe the study of history to be not only the best but the only method for this purpose.] Third, it is, I believe, the fact that most of the fundamental errors currently committed in economic analysis are due to lack of historical experience more often than to any other shortcoming of the economist's equipment. History must of course be understood to include fields that have acquired different names as a consequence of specialization, such as prehistoric reports and ethnology (anthropology).

I personally believe this to be one of the wisest and most profound, as well as most neglected, of Schumpeter's teachings. Taken seriously, the implications would be incredibly far-reaching. The more or less standard economics curriculum of American colleges and universities would have to be radically transformed from beginning to end. Economic history, interpreted in a very broad sense, which has become the stepchild of the profession—if indeed it ranks even that high—would have not only to be restored to the position it occupied forty or fifty years ago but elevated far above that position. In fact it would have to be made the centerpiece of the curriculum around which everything else would be organized. And one final implication of a different sort: by Schumpeter's standard, as set forth in the passage quoted, I am sorry to say that there is really no such thing as scientific economics in this country today. Or perhaps I should say that if scientific economics in his sense does exist, it has escaped my attention.

Please do not misunderstand me. My purpose in beginning on this note is not to criticize or put down. I do not blame the present state of economics on any individuals or groups. It is itself an aspect of an historical process with deep roots and manifold ramifications which I could not even pretend to analyze in the time available to me. My purpose is rather to provide the rationale for the kind of talk I propose to indulge in.

Since I believe that it is history, in both Schumpeter's meanings of "facts" and "sense," which is primarily missing in today's economics, I could not very well fail to use this opportunity to attempt to indicate some of the ways I think the lack could be made good. Let me try then in desperate brevity (to use a favorite expression of Schumpeter) to put "modern capitalism" into a meaningful historical and global perspective.

II

Capitalism as a world system had its origins in the late fifteenth and early sixteenth centuries when Europeans, mastering the art of long-distance navigation, broke out of their little corner of the globe and roamed the seven seas, conquering, plundering, and trading. Ever since then capitalism has consisted of two sharply contrasting parts: on the one hand a handful of dominant exploiting countries and on the other hand a much larger number of dominated and exploited countries. *The two are indissolubly linked together, and nothing that happens in either part can be understood if it is considered in abstraction from the system as a whole.* It is important to stress that this is as true of "modern capitalism," meaning the global capitalist system of the last half of the twentieth century, as it was of the predominantly mercantile capitalism of the period before the Industrial Revolution. In what follows we shall refer to the two parts of the world capitalist system as "developed" and "underdeveloped." We thus do not subscribe to the usage which equates "modern" with "developed." The underdeveloped part of the system is as modern as the developed part.

III

The central dynamic force in the world capitalist system as a whole is the capital accumulation process in the developed countries. It began with what Marx called the primary accumulation of capital, a double process involving: (a) the creation of a wage-labor force, and (b) the amassing of liquid capital. The wage-labor force was created in the main through the expropriation of the peasantry, and a large part of the liquid capital was provided from the loot and profits extracted from the subjugated dependencies. After this stage came the "normal" process of capital accumulation, i.e., the production of surplus value by wage labor, the appropriation of this surplus value by capitalists, and the conversion of a large part of the surplus value into additional capital. The process is by its very nature an expanding one, always requiring new fields for investment, more labor power and raw materials, and larger markets for finished products. Creating conditions favorable to the most rapid accumulation of capital and removing obstacles which impede the process are the central tasks of the capitalist state to which, in the final analysis, all its other functions are subordinated.

In the course of the accumulation process, capital undergoes technological and organizational transformations. The earliest form of capitalist production was what Marx called manufacture (many craftsmen working in a single enterprise with a more or less elaborate specialization and division of labor). Under the impact of the Industrial Revolution (roughly 1750 to 1850 in England), manufacture gave way to machine industry (in which the focus shifts from the worker to the machine and the former becomes increasingly a mere appendage of the latter). The development of machinery and of other advanced technologies in the fields of industry, transportation, and communication made both possible and necessary a steady expansion in the size of the viable unit of capitalist production. The small capitalist proprietorship or partnership which characterized the early stages of development gave way to the corporation, an organizational form which permits an unlimited concentration and centralization of capital, and at the same time gives rise to and in turn is fostered by an increasingly elaborate financial superstructure of banks, securities markets, holding companies, etc.

The concentration, centralization, and corporatization of capital began in earnest in the last third of the nineteenth century and has been proceeding ever since. In the United States, which by the mid-twentieth century had become the leading developed capitalist nation, there were three great waves (interrupted by periods of war or depression): around the turn of the century, in the 1920s, and since the Second World War. By 1962 the 100 largest manufacturing corporations (about .05 percent of all manufacturing corporations) controlled 58 percent of the land, buildings, and equipment used in manufacturing. A similar situation exists in the other developed capitalist countries.

IV

With the growth of the giant corporation, capitalism left its competitive stage and entered its monopoly stage. In the competitive stage individual firms grow by reducing costs, realizing larger profits, and investing in increased capacity to turn out products which, being essentially indistinguishable from the products of rivals, can always be sold at or slightly under the going market price. But as some firms prosper and grow and others lag behind and drop out, the average firm in an industry becomes so large that it must take account of the effect of its own production on market price. It then begins to function more and more like a monopolist, for whom the problem of continued growth is radically transformed. Monopoly profits make possible even more rapid growth than in the past, but the need to maintain monopoly prices dictates a policy of slowing down and carefully regulating the expansion of productive capacity. Given these possibilities and constraints, the result is an irresistible drive on the part of the monopolistic firm to move outside of and beyond its historical field of operation, to penetrate new industries and new markets. Thus the typical production unit in modern developed capitalism is a giant corporation, which is both conglomerate (operating in many industries) and multinational (operating in many countries).

Even in capitalism's competitive stage, the accumulation of capital always tended to outrun the expansion of markets. The result was periodic crises and depressions in which much capital was liquidated or devalued as a necessary prelude to a renewal of the accumulation process. This problem of imbalance between accumulation and expansion of markets is accentuated under monopoly capitalism: as already noted, monopolistic pricing tends to generate both an acceleration of accumulation and a slowing down of the growth of output. The result is that monopoly capitalism is characterized not only by "normal" business cycles but also by a powerful tendency to secular stagnation, such as materialized in the United States in the period 1907-1915 and again with multiplied force in the depression years of the 1930s.

Given the tendency to secular stagnation, the continued existence of monopoly capitalism depends on the existence or creation of sufficiently strong counteracting forces to permit the system to operate at a politically tolerable level of production and employment. In part these forces are generated within the economy itself. In conditions of monopoly, competition among giant corporations is not eliminated; rather it is displaced from the field of price to the field of sales promotion (through advertising, product differentiation and innovation, model changes and other forms of contrived obsolescence, etc.). In this way a huge sales effort builds up which employs a vast amount of unproductive labor and in other ways increases the effective demand for goods and services.

But the sales effort by itself is not enough to neutralize the tendency to stagnation. This therefore becomes increasingly the responsibility of the state which, as noted above, has as its primary task to assure the smooth functioning of the accumulation process. The state can counteract stagnation by suitably large expenditures on welfare and/or warfare, both of which are indispensable to monopoly capitalism for other reasons: welfare as a way of placating the masses and dissuading them from turning to revolutionary politics, and warfare as a means used by each leading capitalist power to maximize its economic "living space" and to control underdeveloped and potentially rebellious dependent countries. Beginning with the period of active preparations for the Second World War and right down to the present, warfare expenditures have clearly been the dominant and, on the whole, sufficient counteracting force preventing the world capitalist system from returning to a state of chronic depression such as characterized most of the decade of the 1930s.

V

In the beginning the relations between the developed and underdeveloped parts of the world capitalist system were based on force. The stronger conquered the weaker, plundered their resources, subjected them to unequal trading relations, and reorganized their economic structures (e.g., by introducing slavery) to serve the needs of the Europeans. In the course of these predatory operations vast colonial empires were built up and fought over by the Spanish, Portuguese, Dutch, French, and British; and the wealth transferred from the colonies to the metropolises was an important factor in the economic development of the latter. Gradually the element of force receded into the background to be replaced by "normal" economic relations of trade and investment—without, however, in any way weakening the basic development/underdevelopment pattern, or stopping the transfer of wealth from the periphery to the center. After its victory in the Napoleonic Wars and the related dissolution of the Spanish and Portuguese empires in the Americas, Britain—which was already industrially far ahead of the other developed countries—moved into a position of virtual monopoly of world trade in manufactured goods. In these circumstances Britain espoused the doctrine of economic liberalism and managed with remarkable success to export it to many other countries, both developed and underdeveloped. The result was to reinforce Britain's economic hegemony and to make the maintenance of formal colonies increasingly unnecessary. The imperialism of capitalism's early youth seemed to have outlived its usefulness: laissez faire and the market could do the job even better.

This situation did not last long, however. Strong capitalist powers were rising to challenge Britain's supremacy: France recovered, Germany united, the United States began to realize its enormous potential, and Japan deliberately discarded its feudal structure to emulate the most developed capitalist nations and at the same time to ward off the threats of subjugation and colonization which were already engulfing China. In all these countries the formation of monopolies in the manner already described proceeded apace; and new technologies in metallurgy, energy production, petroleum, chemicals, etc., gave fresh urgency to the problem of controlling sources of raw materials and markets. The closing decades of the nineteenth century therefore witnessed the upsurge of a new imperialism. All of Africa was partitioned in a few years, and everywhere the developed countries turned increasingly to the use of force to subjugate dependencies, exclude rivals, and pre-empt bases and territory of actual or potential strategic value. Militarism became more and more decisive in all aspects of the life of the dominant powers.

Out of this situation arose the First World War (1914-1918) which had as major consequences for the global capitalist system: (a) extensive reshuffling of colonies and dependencies in favor of the victorious countries; (b) emergence of the United States as economically the strongest capitalist country; (c) socialist revolution in Tsarist Russia, the weakest of the imperialist powers, removing one-sixth of the earth's land surface from the orbit of capitalism and demonstrating to the underdeveloped countries that for them socialist development is a viable alternative to continued capitalist underdevelopment; and (d) birth and/or vigorous growth of national liberation movements in many under-developed countries, for the most part strongly influenced by the Russian Revolution. Thenceforth the dominant capitalist powers had to cope not only with their own internecine struggles but also with challenges from the rival socialist system and from increasingly militant liberation movements in their dependencies.

The Second World War and its outcome faithfully reflected these realities. Started as a war by the "have-not" imperialist powers (Germany, Japan, Italy) to redivide the world, it soon acquired, with the Nazi invasion of the USSR, a capitalism-versus-socialism character as well. For reasons of survival the threatened capitalist powers and the invaded Soviet Union made common cause, defeating the Axis challenge. But there was not and could not be a return to the status quo ante.

Eastern Europe was liberated from Nazi occupation by the Soviet Union and entered the socialist camp. America, enriched by the war while all the other imperialist powers were severely damaged, became the undisputed leader of world capitalism. But perhaps most important of all, national liberation struggles in the underdeveloped world reached new heights. One result was the victory of socialist revolutions in China, North Vietnam, North Korea, and later Cuba. Another was the dissolution of the old colonial empires (except the Portuguese), usually voluntarily undertaken by the mother countries in the hope of heading off the development of genuinely revolutionary movements among the oppressed peoples of the colonies. Nonrevolutionary decolonization resulted in the substitution of neocolonialism for the classical form, and in the passage of large areas of the globe out of the old empires into a new worldwide neocolonial American Empire. This relative weakening of the other imperialist powers, taken together with the socialist and national liberation challenges to the imperialist system as a whole, resulted in the establishment and willing acceptance of U.S. hegemony over the entire capitalist system. Militarily, this meant that the United States had to bear the greater part of the burden of "protecting" the "free world," a function which has already involved two major wars (Korea and Vietnam) and numerous military or police actions in widely scattered parts of the world. The arrangement has not been without important economic advantages for the developed countries of Europe and Japan: relieved of crushing military obligations, they have been able to compete effectively with the United States in world markets largely sustained by American military expenditures both inside and outside the United States. And their giant corporations, though starting later than U.S. corporations in the race to establish production and sales subsidiaries throughout both the underdeveloped and the developed parts of the capitalist world, have given increasing indications in recent times that they have the strength to stay in the race and even to penetrate the United States itself.

VI

Until recently there were few dissenters from the view that the future of capitalism would be determined in the developed countries. If—so the reasoning goes—by means of timely state action in the fields of fiscal and monetary policy and industrial planning, capitalism can be made to work well in the United States, Western Europe, and Japan, and if wise policies of trade, investment, and aid are adopted toward the underdeveloped countries, then not only will capitalism survive in the developed countries but it will enable the underdeveloped countries to attain the status of developed ones. If, on the other hand, these tasks are not successfully carried out, then the classical Marxian predictions of proletarian socialist revolutions in the developed countries will come true. In either case, the fate of capitalism will be decided by and in the developed part of the world system.

Since the Second World War, however, it has become increasingly clear that the principal contradiction in the system, at least in the present historical period, is not *within* the developed part but *between* the developed and underdeveloped parts. As we have already seen, the relations of the one to the other (and the policies which grow out of those relations) are fundamentally exploitative: they perpetuate and deepen the development/underdevelopment pattern rather than ameliorating and eventually eliminating it. Some statistical growth has been achieved in some of the dependent countries (e.g., Mexico, Pakistan, South Korea), but most of the increase has gone to tiny oligarchies, while the condition of the masses has not only not improved but in most cases has actually deteriorated. The much discussed population explosion, irreversible in any near future, aggravates the situation and in fact makes it virtually certain that widespread famine lies ahead. Meanwhile, the peoples of the underdeveloped countries have learned, especially from the experience of China since 1949, that there is a way out of the trap in which they now find themselves caught.

That way out lies through revolutionary national liberation struggles of the kind the people of Indochina are now conducting against the United States. Further such struggles in other parts of Asia, in Latin America, and in Africa seem inevitable, with a similar response from the United States, perhaps joined by the other imperialist countries. It is too soon to attempt to predict the outcome of this generalization of national liberation struggles. Clearly, it might be worldwide atomic warfare, from which no country or system will emerge in viable condition. But even now we can say that a meaningful "victory" for capitalism is exceedingly unlikely. The Vietnam war has already proved that wars of this nature and magnitude cause profound divisions and tensions within the involved developed countries. It seems reasonable to suppose that their continuation and escalation will drive these divisions and tensions to the breaking point. If this should happen, the classical Marxian vision of socialist revolution in the most developed capitalist countries would finally come into its own.

Notes:

1. J. A. Schumpeter, *History of Economic Analysis* (New York: Oxford University Press, 1954), pp. 12-13.

Socio-Cultural Transformation in Developing Countries

First, what is a "developing country"? I take it countries like the United States or Japan or Italy, which are certainly changing rather rapidly, both economically and socio-culturally, are not in the "developing category"—without their ultimate destinations being at all clear, to be sure. Neither are the largest of the socialist countries—or if you prefer, countries in transition between capitalism and social-ism—about which the same can be said. Generally, it seems that the term "developing countries" is used synonymously with "countries of the Third World"—i.e., the countries of Asia, Africa, and Latin America which are neither advanced capitalist nor socialist (transitional) in their structure. These countries, taken together, have something like the following importance in the world as a whole:

This is an abbreviated text of a paper given at the Twenty-Second Congress of the International Institute of Sociology in Rome in September 1969.

15

Percent of World Totals

	Population	Output
Advanced capitalist	20	60
Socialist or transitional	30	30
Third World	50	10
	100	100

These figures suggest that the "developing countries" have a very, very long way to go before they can approach, let alone overtake, the already developed countries. But this is perhaps not so important as the direction in which they are moving. Relatively speaking, are they developing at all? The answer, notoriously I am afraid, is no. I believe it is the fact that the Third World is becoming a *larger* part of the world's population and is accounting for a *smaller* share of the world's output.

Nor are matters much better if we look at absolute levels of development. In most of the Third World, per capita income is increasing very slowly if at all, and there seems to be no doubt that many of the most basic indexes of development—such as calorie and protein intake, literacy, educational levels, etc.—are either stagnant or, in some cases, actually declining.

Why then the name "developing countries"? I suggest that there is no *valid* reason for it. It is, I think, an apologetic and propagandistic term, the origin of which is somewhat obscure but the effect of which is absolutely clear: to hide or disguise an ugly reality from the unwary and the gullible. I believe the term "underdeveloped countries" would be more accurate, and I am sorry to say that even that is not strong enough to describe the reality. The best, most accurate, term I can think of is "underdeveloping countries."

I would like to suggest that the most fruitful work on Third World countries in all the social sciences ought to start by asking how the situation I have been describing came into being. Why the tripartite division: advanced capitalist/ socialist/Third World? Unless we have at least a tentative answer to this question, how can we hope to cope effectively with the question of "socio-cultural transformation"—and not only in the Third World but also in the rest of the globe?

So I am sure you will forgive me, or at least bear with me, if I try to sketch in desperate brevity the lines along which I believe an answer must be sought.

First, let me deal with what, in my opinion, is *not* an answer, despite its being widely espoused by social scientists in the Western countries—and also, I believe, in the Eastern European countries.

The wrong answer in question takes the form of a theory which begins by postulating that throughout most of human history the whole world was underdeveloped in the sense that the Third World is today. Then, some time between four and five centuries ago, a small part of the world, in western and Mediterranean Europe, "took off" into development, leaving the rest standing still at the starting line. These countries and their offshoots, especially in North America, became today's advanced capitalist countries. Revolutions after the two world wars resulted in a certain number of socialist countries which turned their backs on private enterprise and the market and effected *their* take-offs by means of centralized bureaucratic planning. The rest of the world, still left in a state of underdevelopment, watched all this and became possessed of a desire to follow the others into development. There were now two possible models to follow, though some countries have shown a desire to combine the two in various ways.

This theory really underlies the concepts of the Third World—which, however, has largely acquired a new meaning through the work of such writers as Pierre Jalée—and the developing countries. I suggest that the theory is fallacious and misleading from beginning to end.

In the first place, it is a grave error to assume that throughout most of human history the world was underdeveloped in the sense that the Third World is underdeveloped today. If we judge by such criteria as technology, the degree of industrialization, and the productivity of human labor, we can certainly say that the whole world was *un*developed up to a few centuries ago. At the same time, it is necessary to remember that all the major continents produced civilizations which for their times were well developed economically, and in other respects, such as art and religion and philosophy, attained heights which we still marvel at today. It is absurd to picture the world before, say, 1500 A.D. as being in the condition of the Third World today. The truth is—and this is the key to understanding the whole of modern history—that *the underdevelopment of the Third World is the product of the very same historical process which resulted in the development of the advanced capitalist world.* The two, development here and underdevelopment there, are the opposite sides of the very same coin.

From the very beginning, capitalism advanced by subjugating, plundering, and exploiting foreign countries and territories. The result was to transfer wealth from the periphery to the metropolis—on the one hand destroying the old society in the periphery and reorganizing it as a dependent satellite, and on the other hand concentrating the resources necessary for the take-off in the metropolis. This process has been repeated again and again, and for many centuries always on a larger and larger scale. Oliver Cox, in his excellent book *Capitalism as a System,*[1] argues, I think persuasively, that the first capitalist state was Venice. Quite a few Italian city-states—Amalfi, Genoa, Florence—achieved similar capitalist success in the later Middle Ages, as did the Hanseatic League and the Flemish cities. But the scale did not begin to expand toward present-day dimensions until the great discoveries of the fifteenth and sixteenth centuries. The center of capitalist expansion shifted first to Portugal and Spain, then to Holland, and then to Britain and France, which between them finally extended capitalism to the four corners of the globe. Not that this was the end of the process. The second half of the nineteenth century was a particularly active period of capitalist expansion, with the United States and Germany and finally Japan getting into the act, and with all of Africa being subjugated and turned into an appendage of the European metropolises. By the end of the nineteenth century, the whole world had been polarized into a handful of wealthy capitalist countries and a host of colonies and semi-colonies.

Now look what happened to the subjugated countries and regions. In every case where the existing social order was incompatible with or stood in the way of the exploitative activities of the conquerors—and it almost always was incompatible or did stand in the way—the existing order was forcibly transformed or destroyed, with dire consequences for the local inhabitants. In their frantic hunt for gold, the Portuguese and Spanish not only seized all they could lay their hands on but forced the natives into the mines where they perished in droves. The native population of the Caribbean area was quite literally wiped out in two or three generations, and in much of Central and South America the Indians could survive only by retreating into the forests or the mountains. To provide needed labor for mines and plantations, the slave trade grew up and large parts of Africa were turned into a vast hunting ground for slaves. Needless to say, the societies of both slave exporting and slave importing areas were totally transformed. In the Caribbean, Central and South America, and Africa we can see in what may be its purest form the process of capitalist underdevelopment at work. And we can also see the other side of the coin in the amassing of huge fortunes by the slave traders of Liverpool and other English port cities—and by those of France and

New England as well. The generation of underdevelopment took a somewhat different but no less spectacular course in the Far East. The Dutch plundered the Indies and then organized one of the most efficient programs of continuing exploitation in the colonial world. The British in India are probably the most famous case of all. What had been not long before the British appeared on the scene one of the most advanced civilizations in the world was mercilessly robbed and turned into one of the poorest and most backward countries in the world. And the other side of the coin, as always, was the amassing of vast riches in the metropolis. Eric Williams, now Prime Minister of Trinidad and Tobago, said in his brilliant monograph *Capitalism and Slavery*,[2] that the industrial revolution in England was financed from the profits, direct and indirect, of Negro slavery in the West Indies. Brooks Adams, in his famous Cassandra-like work *The Law of Civilization and Decay*,[3] gave the credit to the loot from India. Both were right.

After the conquerors and the looters came the investors, the traders, the bankers, and the administrators and advisors —all those who made it their business to turn the colonies and semi-colonies into lasting sources of profit for the metropolises. As a result of their efforts, a characteristic pattern of economic relations developed between the center and the periphery. The periphery came to specialize in producing raw materials needed in the center and to provide a market for the latter's manufactured goods. Ownership of most of the businesses in the periphery fell into the hands of the capitalists of the center and most of the profits flowed into their pockets. The underdevelopment of the periphery was thus frozen, perpetuated, and deepened, while the center was enabled to continue to develop with the aid of the wealth drained out of its satellites.

Let me digress for a moment here to point out that this fundamental pattern of an exploiting center and an exploited periphery is by no means only an international phenomenon. It also occurs nationally, both within the advanced capitalist countries and within the satellite countries. Throughout U.S. history, for example, the relation between the Northeast and South and West has been essentially a metropolis-colony relation; and we see the same thing very clearly today in a country like Brazil, where the wealth and industry are concentrated in the small Rio – San Paulo – Belo Horizonte triangle, while most of the remainder stagnates in dreadful poverty. Even in the center of the center the same thing is observable: Park Avenue and Harlem are, after all, only a few miles apart; and from the roofs of the luxury apartments of Copacabana in Rio one can see in the *favelas* on the surrounding hillsides some of the worst slums in the world.

Against this background, one can easily see how false and misleading it is to divide the world into the parts which took off into development and those which remained in underdevelopment. Historically speaking, the development of the developed part is the result and counterpart of the underdevelopment of the underdeveloped part. Capitalist development inevitably produces development at one pole and underdevelopment at the other. The advanced capitalist countries and the underdeveloped countries are thus not, repeat not, two separate worlds; they are top and bottom sides of one and the same world.

Once this is clearly grasped, much else falls into place in a coherent and intelligible pattern. In the first place the absurdity of expecting (or hoping) that relations between the advanced and underdeveloped countries will result in the development of the latter becomes obvious. Trade, investment, and aid are precisely the means by which the advanced countries exploit the underdeveloped and maintain them in their underdeveloped condition. In the case of trade, this is fairly widely recognized. The exchange of raw materials for manufactured goods tends to reproduce and perpetuate itself, not to develop into something different. And the tendency of import-export price relationships to move against the primary exporting country in peacetime is notorious. There is absolutely nothing in the trading relationship making for the development of the underdeveloped country: quite the contrary.

The same is true of investment by the center in the periphery, though this would doubtless be quite generally disputed by economists of an orthodox persuasion. There is no time to enter into the theoretical intricacies of foreign investment, but I can cite a few massive statistical facts which would be very hard to explain if foreign investment really did promote development of the underdeveloped countries. The figures to which I refer concern British and American foreign investment, respectively, during their most active periods.

The heyday of British imperialism and of British foreign investment was the half century before the First World War. In the period 1870-1913, Britain invested abroad a net amount of £2.4 billion. That is, the investment abroad by Britons was that much more than foreigners' investment in Britain. That would be equal to about $12 billion, with more than twice today's purchasing power—say, $25 billion today, a lot of money by any standard. But—and here is the catch—during the same period, the income from foreign investment flowing into Britain came to £4.1 billion. In other words, the flow of income *to* Britain exceeded the flow of capital *from* Britain by 70 percent. Who, really, was helping whom to develop?

Or take the tremendous outburst of foreign investment from the United States in the two and a half decades after the Second World War. Here I confine attention to the direct foreign investment of U.S. corporations, by far the most important kind of foreign investment. Figures comparable to those given for Britain are, for the period 1950-1963, as follows: net flow of capital from the United States, $17.4

billion; flow of income to the United States, $29.4 billion. The inflow of income thus exceeded the outflow of capital again by almost exactly 70 percent. Once more one must ask: who is really aiding whom? Can it be that the way to develop a country is to transfer a large part of the economic surplus it produces abroad for the use of others?

As for what is called aid from advanced to underdeveloped countries, which is so often pictured as the open sesame to economic development, the record is all too clear: in general, the more aid the less development. The reasons are numerous. A large part of the aid is of a military nature, supposedly for defense against communist aggression, though everyone knows that these subsidized military machines count for naught in the international power balance and are useful only for maintaining unpopular governments in power. And very little of the economic aid has anything to do with economic development. Much of it is normally drained off corruptly into the pockets of officials, both foreign and American. But more important, it was never even meant to be for development. As D. A. Fitzgerald, long an official of the various U.S. foreign aid agencies, said in an interview with *U.S. News & World Report* (February 25, 1963): "A lot of the criticism of foreign aid is because the critic thought the objective was to get economic growth, and this wasn't the objective at all. The objective may have been to buy a base, or to get a favorable vote in the UN, or to keep a nation from falling apart, or to keep some country from giving the Russians air-base rights—or any one of many other reasons." Almost anything but economic development. The purpose, in other words, is really to maintain the status quo in which the developed countries develop and the underdeveloped countries remain underdeveloped.

Against this background the real meaning of the communist revolutions of the twentieth century becomes clear. They are not some kind of historical accident which creates a new model of economic development according to the ideas of a prophet, good or evil depending on your point of view, named Karl Marx. They are simply the expression of the underdeveloped countries' imperative need to escape from the straitjacket of the international capitalist system in which they long ago became entangled. Once caught in that system, they could only go on underdeveloping. Only outside it could they start developing.

How far those which have escaped have succeeded in achieving real, lasting development—even whether they have really escaped once and for all or whether they may not fall back into the capitalist trap—these are questions to which final answers are not yet available. They are therefore also questions which challenge social scientists.

I hope that in dealing with the underdeveloped countries, social scientists may in the future pay more attention to the general global and historical background, fully recognizing underdevelopment for what it is—the other side of the coin of capitalist development.

Notes:

1. Oliver C. Cox, *Capitalism as a System* (New York: Monthly Review Press, 1964).
2. Eric Williams, *Capitalism and Slavery* (New York: G.P. Putnam, 1966).
3. Brooks Adams, *The Law of Civilization and Decay* (New York: Vintage Books, 1955).

On the Theory
of Monopoly Capitalism

My subject requires no preliminary definitions or explanations. Such, if anyone feels the need of them, can safely be
left to emerge from the discussion itself. But I would like to
make quite explicit at the outset an implication of the title,
that a theory of monopoly capitalism is urgently needed
because of what I consider to be the growing inadequacy of
the kind of economics which is taught in institutions of
higher learning not only in the United States and Britain but
throughout the capitalist world today.

Of the various ways in which this inadequacy could be
illustrated, I will comment on just two. The first is the total
inability of received economics to grasp, let alone explain,
the profound tendency to stagnation which lies at the heart
of present-day capitalism. Consider the situation which
existed in the United States at the end of 1970, presumably
near the end of what has been described by the National
Bureau of Economic Research as the mildest recession of the

This is an abridgement and slight revision of the Marshall Lecture
delivered at Cambridge University, April 21 and 23, 1971.

postwar period. In December 1970, official figures showed:

> Unemployment at 6.2 percent of the labor force
> Utilization of manufacturing capacity at 72.3
>   percent of total

These figures by themselves are enough to indicate an enormous amount of idle human and material resources in the U.S. economy. But everyone knows that the official unemployment figures understate the true amount of unemployment. The question is: by how much?

In an attempt to answer this question my colleague Harry Magdoff and I made what we consider to be a conservative estimate from officially recorded changes in labor force participation rates.[1] The striking fact here is that for the last two decades male labor force participation rates have been declining almost continuously, and much more sharply for blacks than for whites. In certain age groups, notably those of high school and college students on the one hand and those of retirement age on the other, this can be explained by the great increase in higher education enrollments and more adequate provision for old age. But these are evidently not the reasons for the decline in participation rates in the so-called prime age groups from 25 to 65. Here we have to assume either the growth of a new leisure class—made up to a disproportionate degree of blacks!—or, what makes sense, the effective exclusion from the labor market of literally millions of working-age adults who, for lack of education or skill or some other reason, have given up hope of earning a living in the normal way in the U.S. economy today. If we count those excluded from employment in this way as unemployed instead of out of the labor force, as common sense dictates we should, we find that as of December 1970, unemployment stood at 9.1 percent rather than the official figure of 6.2 percent. At the end of 1970, then, we can say that nearly 10 percent of the labor force and more than a quarter of manufacturing production were idle in the world's most highly developed capitalist country.

Some of us have been saying for a long time now that if it weren't for the enormous military outlays of today, the U.S. economy would be as profoundly depressed as it was during the Great Depression of the 1930s. Can this assertion be supported by evidence? I think it can. Let us add to the unemployed as just calculated (7.9 million), the following:

	in millions
Members of the armed forces	2.9
Civilian employees of the defense department	1.2
Employees in defense industries	3.0
Those employed because of indirect effects of military spending (multiplier = 1)	7.1

Thus, using conservative estimates where estimates are necessary, the total number of unemployed plus the military and military-dependent employed comes to 22.1 million as of December 1970. This works out to 25.6 percent of the labor force including armed forces. For comparison, the highest unemployment rate ever recorded was 24.9 percent at the depth of the Depression in 1933.

I realize, of course, that there are those who will say that all this has to do with the United States and not with the other advanced capitalist countries. I have no time to argue the point, so I will only ask them to reflect on what would be the consequence for the capitalist world as a whole—including both its developed and its underdeveloped parts—if by far its largest single unit were to be plunged into a deep depression comparable to that of the 1930s.

As far as the United States itself is concerned, it is quite clear that the stagnationist tendency which we have been discussing underlies or contributes to the seriousness of practically all of the country's most critical problems, and in particular the interrelated racial and urban crises. A rough index of the growing seriousness of these problems is the rapidly expanding welfare rolls of America's great cities. Between the 1960 and 1970 censuses, the total population of the United States rose by 13 percent. The population on welfare in the same period shot up by 94 percent. Six percent of all the inhabitants of the United States, the richest country the world has ever known, are now on welfare: 15 percent of the inhabitants of New York, its richest city; 25 percent of the inhabitants of Newark, perhaps its most depressed and disoriented city.

Closely related to these problems is another which I may call the quality of life in the world's most advanced capitalist society. This is something which evidently defies exact description or measurement, but which is no less real on that account. There are many aspects which could be singled out, but it seems to me that perhaps the most compelling is the fearful tensions and conflicts which beset everyday life. Charles Reich, whose book *The Greening of America*[2] is often as strong on description as it is weak on diagnosis, speaks with little exaggeration of "the atmosphere of anxiety and terror in which we all live." And my friend Grace Lee Boggs who lives in Detroit described what I mean with eloquence and passion in a recent lecture at Wayne State University:

> Finally, instead of being a dream, "our present industrial society" is literally becoming a nightmare. For the vast majority of people—not only the Third World peoples living in the inner cities which have been abandoned by the rising working class, but also for the great majority of white workers and middle classes who have been able to buy comfortable homes in the suburbs—the world in which they move about from day to day is one in which the behavior of nothing and no

one, including oneself, is really predictable; where the slightest crack in the system of complexly integrated operations causes chaos; where danger and insecurities lurk on all sides; where carrying out the most mundane yet vital tasks—such as going to the store for a loaf of bread, or coming home from work in a public conveyance, or deciding where to send your child to school, or making a phone call in a phone booth, or asking somebody to do a routine favor or for directions on how to get somewhere—have become struggles for survival, where day after day your insides are constantly sweating it out, even when outwardly you appear to be calm. Having a good job "in our present industrial society" and earning the wherewithal to purchase practically anything you want, have not brought or bought a sense of security and confidence. If anything, it has increased the sense of insecurity and helplessness. This is especially true of a city, like New York, but it is becoming increasingly true of every other city in the U.S.A. where over two-thirds of the American people live.

I suppose most economists will shrug at such descriptions of everyday life in the United States. "Too bad," I can hear them saying, "but what has all that got to do with us?" Well, maybe it hasn't anything to do with them, but I suggest that if this is really true, they mustn't be surprised or offended if more and more people, especially younger people, find them increasingly irrelevant—or, perhaps worse, hypocritical or even fraudulent. For, whatever economists may like to think about it, the quality of life is profoundly involved with economics, and any science worthy of the name will sooner or later have to accept the responsibility which this implies.

It is not my primary purpose, however, to serve up a critique of received economics. That can perhaps come with better grace and more conviction from inside the profession than from outside—and I must confess that, despite a proper initiation and the customary seven years' apprenticeship, I now feel much more outside than inside the economics profession. Nevertheless, I would like to make it clear that all efforts at a serious critique originating within the profession, and even those critiques which remain within it, have my hearty support. It is surely a real step forward to have shown, as has been done here in Cambridge in recent years, that neoclassical economic theory, even considered as an abstract system on its own terms, suffers from fatal logical flaws. Relentless criticism from within is necessary, and it may well be still in its early stages. But it is no substitute for an effort to come to grips with the reality which received economics has so clearly neglected or ignored.

What alternative approaches to this late capitalist reality are there? Without in any way attempting to be exhaustive, I suggest that they can be grouped under three headings which can be conveniently referred to as (a) heterodox bourgeois, (b) traditional Marxist, and (c) neo-Marxist. (I hold no brief for these labels, but up to now at any rate more adequately descriptive ones have not occurred to me.)

The heterodox bourgeois tradition goes back a long way and includes numerous variants. What they have in common is an acceptance of the basic framework of the system, together with an open mind about desirable reforms within this framework. In earlier times there was a good deal of overlapping and intermingling with classical and neoclassical economics. John Stuart Mill can perhaps be taken as the prototype here—a classicist, neoclassicist, and reformer all bound up in one—you might say the last classicist, the first neoclassicist, and the first Fabian. Marshall and Pigou— especially Pigou—were in this tradition. In their hands welfare economics took shape as a genuine critique of capitalist society. It was only later that welfare economics was turned into a set of formal exercises devoid of any real social

content. The procedure here is typical: an apparent effort to
be more precise and concrete led away from, not toward,
reality and relevance. Pigou, it seems to me, ought to be
recognized as one of the important precursors, if not actual
founders, of the modern ecological movement.

But the capitalism against which their criticisms were
aimed was essentially that of the nineteenth rather than the
twentieth century. The large corporation hardly appears, and
monopoly is treated as a special case, not as a phenomenon
typical of the system as a whole. The first explicit recognition by bourgeois economists of twentieth-century capitalist
realities tended to be highly empirical. The growth of
corporations and trade unions, hence of monopolistic elements in the goods and labor markets, the increasing and
changing role of governments in economic affairs—all this was
described and documented in a voluminous literature which
dates from the closing decades of the nineteenth century. But
since there was hardly any place for these developments in
traditional economic theory, this literature was largely
nontheoretical, or even antitheoretical. American institu-
tionalism of the period after the First World War conforms to
this pattern and was the most self-conscious effort up to then
to overthrow what many younger economists of the time felt
as the tyranny of orthodox economic doctrine. But their
efforts to put something in its place—insofar as such efforts
were made at all—were feeble and soon fizzled out.

If I were asked to date the beginnings of a distinctively
bourgeois theory of the capitalist system as it has taken shape
in the twentieth century, I think I would cite Schumpeter's
article "The Instability of Capitalism" which appeared in the
Economic Journal (September 1928). There we not only find
the giant corporation or trust as a characteristic feature of
the system; even more important, this economic unit, so
foreign to the whole corpus of classical and neoclassical
theory, provides the basis for new and important theoretical

propositions. It will be recalled that in the Schumpeterian theory as set forth in *The Theory of Economic Development*,[3] innovation is the function of the individual entrepreneur and that it is from the activity of innovating entrepreneurs that all the dynamic features of the system are directly or indirectly derived. These features include interest on money (absent from Schumpeter's "circular flow"), the operations of the credit system, and the form of the business cycle. In "The Instability of Capitalism," however, Schumpeter places the innovative function no longer in the individual entrepreneur but in the big corporation. At the same time innovation is reduced to a routine carried out by teams of specialists educated and trained for their jobs. In the Schumpeterian scheme of things, these are absolutely basic changes destined to produce equally basic changes in capitalism's *modus operandi*. In "The Instability of Capitalism," he concentrated on what he took to be the implications for the business cycle.

In *Capitalism, Socialism and Democracy*[4] Schumpeter developed this line of thought in a somewhat more sociological than economic direction by present-day academic standards, but it could hardly be said that he made any effort to construct a comprehensive theory of monopoly capitalism.

Schumpeter's initiative attracted little attention, and it was not until after the Second World War that a bourgeois economist again felt challenged to attempt to square an increasingly anachronistic theory with the more and more intrusive facts of twentieth-century capitalism. This time it was J. K. Galbraith who undertook the task, first in his book *American Capitalism*,[5] followed by two other complementary works, *The Affluent Society*[6] and *The New Industrial State*.[7] Since Galbraith is—at least so it seems to me—the leading representative today of what I have called the heterodox bourgeois tradition, and since many of you have had an opportunity this year to become acquainted with his ideas at first hand, a brief critical digression may be in order.

Galbraith is acutely aware of the utter unreality of the assumptions which underlie neoclassical theory, in particular the assumption which, in spite of all disclaimers, is the cornerstone of the whole edifice—a macrosystem of atomistically competitive and essentially self-regulating markets. For all the attention that has been paid to monopolistic elements in the last forty years—since the almost simultaneous publication of the books by Joan Robinson and E. H. Chamberlin—there has never been any attempt by neoclassical economics to relate them to the functioning of the system as a whole. Here I believe Galbraith is on absolutely solid ground, and I do not see how he can be seriously challenged when he writes (in *The New Industrial State*) that "economics as it is conventionally taught, is in part a system of belief designed less to reveal truth than to reassure its communicants about established social arrangements."

Galbraith shows a fine disdain for all the theoretical models and constructs of orthodox theory—innocent games at best, deliberate obfuscation at worst. Instead, he presents us with what is perhaps the first attempt at a theory of an economic system dominated by giant corporations. In broad outline, it runs more or less as follows (I am subject to correction, of course): The heart of the big corporation is modern technology which involves greater specialization, more trained manpower, and much larger amounts of capital than in the past. More time is now needed to work up a new project and bring it into full operation. It is more difficult and expensive to shift from one project to another. Decision-making thus becomes more complex and more risky. The only way to cope with such complexity and risk is to plan. Planning, however, has its own inherent logic. To plan effectively, the corporation must be able to control its own destiny, independently of control by outside financial institutions. A steady and secure flow of profits must therefore be available to finance research and development and expansion. Such a profit goal is attainable only if the corporation can, first, control markets and manipulate customers so that enough goods are sold at the right prices; and second, control necessary supplies, raw materials, etc., at consistent prices. But the giant corporation, for all its independence and power, would still be vulnerable without an adequate and steady flow of consumer demand and consequently consumer income. This is where government enters the economic picture, initiating and guaranteeing a huge spending program which, as Galbraith sees it, inevitably centers on military supplies and preparations. To quote what seems to me a key passage (from *The New Industrial State*): "If a large public sector of the economy, supported by personal and corporate income taxation, is the fulcrum for the regulation of demand, plainly military expenditures are the pivot on which the fulcrum rests. Additionally, they provide underwriting for advanced technology and therewith, security for the planning of the industrial system in areas that would otherwise be excluded by cost and risk."

What Galbraith takes to be the logical necessity of these arrangements produces a seemingly harmonious blending of the goals of business, labor, and government. The center of power is *not* top management but what Galbraith calls the "technostructure," which includes the whole range of executives, sub-executives, technicians, and other specialists who participate in group decision-making. The interests of the technostructure lie in the success of the corporation. The aim is therefore no longer, as in the case of the old-fashioned entrepreneur, maximum profits, but security and growth. Enough profits have to be made to pay dividends and to create an independent fund for research and investment, but the major emphasis is on maximizing the growth of sales. Given planning and growth, a benevolent attitude toward trade unions becomes both possible and desirable. Thus the industrial technostructure and the bureaucracies of government and unions tend to be merged into what might be called a single interest group. From a purely economic point of view, according to Galbraith, this system works very well indeed, producing a hitherto unimaginable degree of affluence. But it has its drawbacks, chief of which are: First, the key role of military spending in managing demand and stimulating technological advance creates a military interest which has to justify itself by cold and hot wars. This is a standing danger which could lead to disaster. Second, apart from the military, the system regularly underestimates and undersupplies public and collective needs. Thus alongside private affluence it produces public squalor. And third, the system has no place for nonmaterial and noncommercial values: it tends to create an aesthetic and moral wasteland. In Galbraith's view, however, these faults can be remedied by political action. The question is whether the system also creates a political interest with the actual or potential power to undertake the required action. And here Galbraith closes the circle. Modern technology, which ultimately dominates the whole thing—Galbraith is very much a technological determinist—necessitates a vast expansion in the number of scientists and educators, and these are supposed to be the very people who can save the system from its own destructive tendencies. In the final analysis, then, the New Industrial State turns out to be hardly less a harmonious and self-equilibrating system than the utopia of free competition it replaces. It begins with what seems like hardheaded realism about the big corporation, modern technology, the corporate state, and so on; but it ends up about as far removed as any other brand of bourgeois social science from the grim world

of stagnation, poverty, urban decay and crisis, racial discrimination and exploitation, imperialism and war, which stares
out at us through the headlines of every day's newspaper.

Where does Galbraith go wrong?

Basically, I think, in denying the essential class character
of his corporate society. The trick here is the technostructure
which is supposed to be the real power and which is pictured
as choosing its goals independently of the property owner's
undeniable urge to maximize profits. The whole thing is, of
course, an illusion which has been exposed many times but
which reappears in one form or another with the regularity of
the hardiest weed.

I always like to appeal to reputable authority when I can
do so with a good conscience, and this is one of the fortunate
occasions when that is possible. In a lecture delivered at the
New School for Social Research in New York last month
(March 1971), Paul Samuelson, of textbook and Nobel Prize
fame, spoke as follows:

> I find Galbraith's notion that there is a technostruc-
> ture which really runs our corporations, government,
> and which represents a convergence of form and
> function with the technostructure which runs Russia
> and China, to be a notion bred in part out of
> exaggerated self-esteem. I'd like to think that our MIT
> students will inherit the earth ... but reality keeps
> breaking in. They, like the large corporation itself, are
> constitutional monarchs who reign only so long as they
> don't rule. Just let some computer tell Henry Ford, or
> for that matter the General Motors Board, that they've
> got to do something he [the computer] wants but
> which they [Henry Ford or the GM Board] don't think
> is in their long-run interest, and see how fast he draws
> his severance pay.

What Samuelson is saying, in a nutshell, is that the
technostructure is hired and fired by top management, and

that what defines the boss is precisely the power to hire and fire. This is a basic truth which one wishes all economists—and other social scientists as well—could firmly grasp and retain.

Once the myth of the independent technostructure is disposed of, one can go about the business of debunking the rest of the Galbraithian system of social harmonics. Stagnation, unemployment, racial discrimination, urban decay, and all the other ugly features of present-day capitalist reality can be explained—rather than explained away—as the natural result of profit maximization in monopolistic markets. Wars like that in Indochina, which is literally tearing to pieces the fabric of U.S. society, can be recognized not as "mistakes" or antics of an unruly military establishment but as grim efforts of the capital-owning class to preserve at all costs the overseas markets and sources of raw materials which are increasingly vital elements in the profit-making potential of the giant corporations. (For Galbraith not even to have mentioned this aspect must have required a quite remarkable degree of self-control, since he does stress the importance for corporate planning of control over markets and supplies, and there is no reason to suppose that a corporation would willingly exempt foreign markets and sources of supply from its planning horizon just because they happen to be outside a particular set of national boundaries.)

So much, then, for heterodox bourgeois approaches to the realities of present-day capitalism. They are interesting and have their value, both positive and negative. But naturally enough they always stop short of challenging and criticizing the system itself, and this in the final analysis is their fatal weakness.

Turning now to the Marxist approaches, I have distinguished two varieties—traditionalist Marxist and neo-Marxist.

I am not going to spend much time on the first, chiefly because I don't believe the traditional Marxists have made

significant contributions to a theory of monopoly capitalism.[8] They have their economic theory from *Capital* which
they seem to consider equally applicable to the capitalism of
today as it was to the capitalism of the mid-nineteenth
century. Of course they are aware that Marx had a theory of
the concentration and centralization of capital, and they
often cite this as evidence of the superiority of Marxian
economics. Marx, they say, predicted the coming of monopoly capitalism, but that's about as far as they go. If
monopoly capitalism itself requires any new theories, or
reformulations of old ones, the traditional Marxists are silent
about the matter.

On another level, the traditionalists of course embrace
Lenin's theory of imperialism with its emphasis on monopoly
and state action, but there is no effort to integrate this
theory with the economics Marx expounded in the three
volumes of *Capital*. And when it comes to the features which
most strikingly differentiate the capitalism of Marx's day
from that of our own, the traditionalists usually do not get
much beyond commonplace description. I refer here to giant
corporations and resultant monopolistic market situations,
the various types of state intervention into the economy, the
different forms of imperialist domination and dependence,
the manipulation of consumption, the attempted creation by
mass media of pliable consumers and producers—all these
things are recognized to exist, but they find no theoretical
expression in traditionalist Marxism. The reason, I suppose, is
that the traditional Marxists believe that whatever has
happened or could happen under capitalism is in some way
accounted for in the basic texts and that to admit the need
for new theoretical departures is already a form of revisionism.

None of this is to deny that traditionalist Marxism is in
many respects a powerful tool for interpreting present-day
capitalist reality. Much about capitalism *is* unchanged since

Marx's day, and still more since Lenin's. Classes, exploitation, class struggle—the forms change but the substance remains. And those who see and interpret capitalism in these terms—whether it be the capitalism of the nineteenth century or the twentieth century—are almost sure to be able to comprehend and explain much more than any bourgeois social scientists. But this is not to say that traditionalist Marxism has made significant contributions to understanding what is specific to monopoly capitalism. In my opinion, it has not.

As to neo-Marxist approaches, I should first reiterate what I said earlier, that I am not particularly wedded to the label. I use it not to designate a group which is in some sense less genuinely Marxist than others—though clearly some may be—but rather a group which is less convinced of the adequacy of Marxist theory as it has been inherited from the past.

One of the first big steps toward a real theory of monopoly capitalism was taken by Kalecki when he introduced what he called "the degree of monopoly" into an analysis of the capitalist accumulation process. (I do not think it matters much whether we count Kalecki as a Marxist or not. Clearly he was not a traditional Marxist, but I think a case could be made that he was sufficiently influenced by Marxism to be classified a neo-Marxist, as I am using the term. But the important thing from our present point of view is that Kalecki's introduction of monopoly into the analysis of the accumulation process has, so to speak, been appropriated by neo-Marxism, while being ignored by bourgeois economics, probably because its implications are basically thoroughly radical.)

Let us pause here to review very briefly Marx's theory of the accumulation process. Capitalists hire workers at wages which are equal to the value of labor power. The value of labor power in turn is determined, not as in the case of classical economics by a physical subsistence minimum, but by a historically conditioned conventional standard of living. I think the implication is that the extent to which this conventional minimum exceeds basic subsistence is determined in the final analysis by the cumulative effect of past class struggles. But as of any given period, this is a datum. Considering the important role it plays in the whole theory, this question of the determination of the value of labor power receives remarkably little attention from either Marx or his followers.

Having hired workers at the value of their labor power, capitalists put them to work with machines and raw materials which of course belong to the capitalists. Let us suppose that the average workday is ten hours and that in the first five hours the workers turn out a product with a value equal to their wages. What they produce in the remaining five hours then belongs to the capitalists and accrues to them as surplus value. The workers of course consume their wages, or rather the consumer goods which they buy with their wages. The capitalists consume only part of their surplus value, devoting the rest to accumulation. The accumulated part is divided between buying more labor power and buying more machines and materials. In this way the reproduction process continually expands through the production and investment of larger and larger amounts of surplus value.

If all went smoothly, this process could go on forever. But Marx argued that it couldn't proceed smoothly, that various kinds of obstacles and roadblocks would inevitably develop. One of these blockages, not fully worked out by Marx, was an inappropriately high rate of accumulation relative to the growth of consumption which would cause a breakdown of the accumulation process.

If we insert monopoly into this model, what is the result? If the value of the labor power is taken as an irreducible magnitude, clearly the only effect of monopoly will be redistribution of surplus value from more competitive to more monopolistic sectors. Even this, however, can increase the rate of accumulation—since it concentrates surplus value in fewer hands, and those who receive more accumulate a larger proportion than those who receive less—and thus hasten the emergence of overaccumulation problems. Kalecki went a step further, arguing that monopoly would not only *concentrate* surplus value but also *increase the amount* of surplus value at the expense of wages. This need not be interpreted to mean an actual *reduction* of wages; it can mean slower growth of wages than would have taken place in the absence of monopoly. And if monopoly is not only introduced as a once-and-for-all factor but as a secularly growing force, then the whole capital accumulation process can be permanently and increasingly biased toward over-accumulation and stagnation.

As usual with Kalecki, this line of thought was presented with utmost terseness, occupying altogether no more than a paragraph or two.[9] But the theme was taken up by Steindl, who was a colleague of Kalecki at Oxford during the war. Steindl developed the theme into a powerful treatise entitled *Maturity and Stagnation in American Capitalism*[10] which I think is both one of the most important and most neglected works of political economy of the last half century.

The question which Steindl set out to answer was why the American economy remained in a state of deep depression during the whole decade of the 1930s. Others had attempted answers at the time, most notably Hansen and Schumpeter, but neither they nor Marxist writers of the period could propose an explanation which showed the Great Depression to be a logical outcome of the functioning of the capitalist system. This is just what Steindl did do. He demonstrated that the growth of monopoly, already fully anticipated and explained in Marx's theory of the concentration and central-ization of capital, must have a powerful retarding effect on the capital accumulation process, and this in turn could only mean an ever deepening tendency to stagnation. The 1930s saw these inherent forces and tendencies of capitalism finally rise to the surface to dominate the economic scene.

With this, it seems to me that the foundations of a sound and essentially Marxist theory of monopoly capitalism were firmly laid. The logic is beautiful in its unity and coherence: competition inevitably gives way to monopoly via the concentration and centralization of capital, and monopoly retards the accumulation process, giving rise to ever more powerful tendencies to stagnation.

This, however, is of course no more than the foundation of a theory of monopoly capitalism. Quite apart from its effects on the accumulation process, the growth of monopoly and its institutional forms (the giant corporation and the financial system that goes with it) has far-reaching consequences. And, no less important, the protective reaction of the system, both as a whole and in various of its parts, to the threats inherent in chronic stagnation force new functions and behavior patterns on almost all sectors of the society, political as well as economic.

I cannot aspire to anything like a comprehensive discussion of these subjects, and not only for lack of time. No less important is the fact that while there is a large descriptive literature dealing with various aspects, there is still not very much in the way of real theoretical analysis. There is a great deal of work to be done here, and it seems to me that the younger political economists who will have to do it have been rather slow in setting about the job. Let me make a few suggestions.

In the first place it seems clear to me that we need a new theory of the firm. The earlier economists were very much concerned with this problem, Marshall in particular. Marshall had what might be called a biological theory of the firm. Operating in essentially competitive markets, firms are born, grow to maturity, move on to senility, and finally die. At any given time an industry, which of course was thought of as producing an essentially homogeneous commodity, is made up of firms in all stages of growth and decline. It was to deal with this situation theoretically that Marshall invented the concept of the representative firm. Representative firms are perhaps best thought of as those in the prime of life which, taken together, constitute the bulk of an industry. Marshall believed that in analyzing cost and supply conditions in an industry, one could legitimately confine attention to a representative firm, a device which enormously simplifies what might otherwise be an unmanageably complicated problem. Whether or not this device can be said to have worked is surely debatable, but this should not obscure the fact that it was not dreamed up out of thin air. If one reads, for example, G. C. Allen's classic description of the organization of production in Birmingham and the Black Country around the middle of the nineteenth century, one can see very clearly the empirical basis of Marshall's thinking on the firm. Competition and the life-cycle conception of the firm were both realities. Nineteenth-century realities, of course.

Marxism from the outset pointed to a different theory of the firm. Here we have to start with the key Marxian idea, quite consistent with Ricardian theory but equally foreign to neoclassical theory, that *every unit of capital is inherently and necessarily an expanding unit*. This follows from the very nature of capital as self-expanding value. Allow me to quote two passages from *Capital* which clarify the logic of this absolutely basic principle of Marxian economics:

The exact form of this process is . . . M–C–M′, where M′ = M + △M = the original sum advanced plus an increment. This increment or excess over the original value I call "surplus value." The value originally advanced therefore not only remains intact while in circulation, but adds to itself a surplus value or expands itself. It is this movement that converts it [money] into capital. . . .

The circulation of money as capital is . . . an end in itself, for the expansion of value takes place only within this constantly renewed movement. The circulation of capital has therefore no limits. . . . The expansion of value, which is the objective basis or mainspring of the circulation M–C–M, becomes his [the capitalist's] subjective aim. . . . Use value must therefore never be looked upon as the real aim of the capitalist; neither must the profit on any single transaction. The restless never-ending process of profit-making alone is what he aims at.[11]

This points not to a biological theory of the firm but to what might be called an explosion theory. Only of course not all firms can go on growing forever. This is where the theory of concentration and centralization of capital comes in. Like trees in a young forest, some firms grow faster than others. The laggards are stunted and eventually choked to death, giving the survivors more room to grow in. In many cases—and here the tree analogy fails—the bigger and stronger take over and incorporate the smaller. Eventually, the number is reduced to the point where competition gives way to monopoly (I use the term "monopoly" in a broad sense to include the various forms and stages of oligopoly).

When this stage is reached, the firm undergoes a characteristic transformation. According to well-known principles of microeconomics—which I believe should be perfectly acceptable to Marxism—the monopolist no longer maximizes his profit by producing to the point where marginal cost equals price but to the point where marginal cost equals marginal revenue. This implies lower output, higher price, and higher profit. It does not, however, mean any lessening of the urge to expand. The problem for the firm is now different. On the one hand, it must be careful not to expand in a way to spoil its own market. On the other hand, its increased profits make possible more rapid expansion than ever (either through direct investment of profits, or through making use of improved access to outside funds, or some combination). There is an apparent contradiction here: reduced scope for expansion *versus* increased ability to expand.

The resolution of this contradiction becomes the key to the understanding of firm behavior in the period of monopoly capitalism. The basic principle can be stated this way: to continue to expand freely, that is to say, in accordance with its capabilities, the firm must transcend its history. It was born and grew up producing and selling a certain product in a certain region. It must learn to overcome both these historical limitations. It must, in other words, strive to acquire new markets in both the product and the geographical senses. The one necessity leads to conglomeration, the other more or less directly to various forms of multinationalism.

Certain implications of this analysis of the firm should be noted. In the monopoly phase, two of economic theory's oldest and most time-honored axioms no longer hold. There is no longer a tendency for profit rates to converge toward a system-wide average rate of profit. The determination of the profit rate accruing to the producer of a particular product is a complicated problem which I don't want to go into now—costs, demand (including rate of growth of demand), and conditions of entry all play a part. The point is that there is no theoretical or factual reason to suppose that there is a tendency to equality as between products, or between firms—or even for that matter between the different divisions of a single firm. There are many different profit rates. In the United States during the 1950s, for example, for nineteen manufacturing industry groups the range was from a low of 10.32 percent for textile mill products to a high of 24.41 percent for transport equipment (which includes automobiles), with a wide variety of rates in between. Nor was the United States in any way exceptional. In the other countries studied by Minhas (United Kingdom, Japan, Canada, India), similar spreads existed, although the relative position of industries varied from country to country.[12]

One can of course average these rates, for one country or for all, but the result is nothing more than a number devoid of operational significance. To be sure, to the extent that there is a competitive sector in a monopoly capitalist economy—which means more or less standardized products and minimum capital requirements for entry—there is a meaningful average rate of profit *for that sector;* and this is no doubt a factor of considerable importance in the functioning of monopoly capitalism. But it should not be allowed to obscure the fact that the overall average *rate* of profit—though of course not the total *volume* of profit—does not have the significance attaching to it in conditions of competition.

A corollary of this of course is that if the average rate of profit has no operational significance, then neither does a rise or a fall in the average rate of profit. It may still be possible to have a theory about the significance of rising and declining profit rates, substituting frequency distributions for averages. But to my knowledge, no attempts in this direction have been made.

Another implication of the theory of the firm sketched here is that capital can move from higher to lower profit-rate areas as well as vice versa. What counts for the monopolistic firm seeking outlets for its investible profits (and/or borrowings) is not whether the rate of profit it can earn in another area is higher than what it is earning now, but whether the profit rate on an *additional* investment in the new area is higher or lower than that on an additional investment in its present field of activity. To put the matter quite concretely—without, I think, losing any generality—if General

Motors has $100 million to invest, it will not decide whether to invest it in additional automobile capacity or in, say, additional refrigerator capacity by comparing the rate of profit in its auto division with that in its Frigidaire division. To put more into autos might actually involve a reduction in profit even though the current rate of profit there is—as indeed it often is—over 25 percent. And if Frigidaire—and all the other two dozen or more industries in which General Motors is a major producer—are in a similar condition, well, General Motors may decide just to invest in U.S. Treasury bonds unless or until something new and attractive (i.e., with a prospective yield higher than that of Treasury bonds) comes along.

This ability of capital to flow the "wrong way," i.e., from areas of higher to areas of lower return, will perhaps distress those who are accustomed to explaining phenomena—particularly imperialist phenomena—by profit-rate differentials, falling tendencies of profit rates, etc. Actually, I think there is no loss. Such explanations are simply irrelevant under monopoly capitalism, and it is better they should be abandoned. Nor does this leave us without valid explanatory principles. As Oskar Lange wrote some forty years ago: "The pursuit of surplus monopoly profits suffices to explain completely the imperialistic nature of present-day capitalism. Consequently, special theories of imperialism which resort to artificial constructions, such as Rosa Luxemburg's theory . . . are quite unnecessary."[13] I need only add that theories of imperialism which rely on profit-rate comparisons fall under the same stricture. But I think Lange's statement should be amended to say not that such theories are unnecessary but that they are wrong. (Oskar Lange, incidentally, was, like his fellow countryman Michal Kalecki, an economist who was perfectly familiar with and indeed made notable contributions to the methods and achievements of bourgeois economics. Neither man hesitated to use whatever he found valuable in this tradition; and yet neither man was over-whelmed or trapped by it. Their basic orientation was and remained Marxian and socialist. They provide, it seems to me, admirable examples for the younger generation of radical economists in the West.)

Before I leave this subject, let me add that what Lange calls the "pursuit of surplus monopoly profits" could well be taken as the starting point for a comprehensive investigation of the whole range of topics, political as well as economic, that commonly fall under the heading of imperialism. It is only necessary to add that the term "pursuit" must be interpreted in a broad sense to include not only chase and capture but also all subsequent arrangements to secure and perpetuate. As Galbraith so often insists—and it is unques-tionably one of the strongest points of his theory—the modern giant corporation has a profound need to *dominate and control* all the conditions and variables which affect its viability. And this explains so much of what seems merely irrational or perverse to one steeped in abstract neoclassical modes of thought. It explains why, for example, the giant corporation, as soon as it feels strong enough to do so, typically moves from export to production abroad, and why it strives with might and main to control, directly or in concert with other giant corporations, governments wherever it operates.

Allow me now to return to a subject which I introduced earlier but did not follow up. I asserted—or, if you prefer, proposed the hypothesis—that underlying the whole develop-ment of modern monopoly capitalism is a profound tendency to stagnation. (The Keynesians would call it a chronic deficiency of effective demand; and I think some of them are convinced that it really exists, though as far as I know none has made any serious attempt in recent years to explain why.) I then went on to suggest that this tendency to stagnation provokes or strengthens a whole series of protective reactions. It was this range of phenomena with which Paul Baran and I were largely—though by no means exclusively—concerned in our book, *Monopoly Capital*. I have no desire or intention to expound the arguments of that effort, but I would like to take the occasion to look, very briefly and cursorily, at some of the objections that have been raised to the conceptual apparatus which Baran and I employed.

If you will recall my earlier sketch of the Marxian theory of accumulation, you will remember that I located the source of the tendency to stagnation in overaccumulation in relation to the growth of consumption. Since accumulation is assumed to take place exclusively from surplus value, this amounts to saying that the problem concerns the magnitude and modes of utilization of surplus value. In the simplest (most abstract) model, the determinants are (a) the value of labor power or real wages, (b) the productivity of labor, (c) the division of surplus value between the capitalists' consumption and accumulation, and (d) the division of accumulation between variable and constant capital. This is, however, a very simplified or abstract scheme, and it should not be taken to mean that there was no room in Marx's theory for other modes of utilization of surplus value. Three in particular were clearly recognized by Marx.

First, the upkeep of the state apparatus. Given the assumption of a fixed and irreducible real wage, there is of course no other possible source of tax revenue than surplus value.

Second, the incomes of unproductive workers, of which domestic servants were not only typical but in Marx's time also the most numerous group. (State employees were of course also unproductive workers, but of a different sort, supported indirectly rather than directly from the surplus value accruing to capitalists. In general, for Marx, productive labor is that which *creates* surplus value; unproductive labor, that which is *supported from* surplus value.)

Third, what Marx called "expenses of circulation." Here I would like to quote what I think is the key passage, which comes from Volume II of *Capital* and is less likely to be familiar than the well-known formulations of Volumes I and III.

> The general law is that *all expenses of circulation, which arise only from changes of form, do not add any value to the commodities.* They are merely expenses required for the realization of value, or its conversion from one form into another. The capital invested in those expenses (including the labor employed by it) belongs to the dead expenses of capitalist production. They must be made up out of the surplus product and are, from the point of view of the entire capitalist class, a deduction from the surplus value or surplus product.[14]

It seemed to Baran and me—and still seems to me—that this provides the needed conceptual framework to bring the whole problem of selling costs within the framework of Marxian theory.

Now Marx in his day believed that the essentials of the capitalist process could best be highlighted and analyzed by abstracting from what he considered to be these secondary forms of utilization of surplus value. I think he was undoubtedly right. But I think it is equally clear that this is no longer true today. Not only have the sales effort and state expenditures increased enormously, but they are precisely the channels and instruments through which the system reacts in attempting to protect itself against the destructive consequences of the underlying tendency to stagnation. To abstract from these factors *now* is to commit the least excusable of scientific sins, that is, to ignore what is essential to an understanding of the segment of reality under study. The fact that bourgeois social science commits this sin all the time, and indeed seems to regard it as a positive virtue, is no reason why Marxists should follow the same course.

I have no time to elucidate the dynamic processes here. Suffice it to say two things: First, that the new forms of competition, which under conditions of monopoly replace the older forms of price competition, put an entirely new emphasis on the arts of salesmanship, and that the sales effort, in turn, both reacts back on the economic process and creates a distinctive monopoly-capitalist culture. Second, that the growing need for modes of utilization of surplus value other than capital accumulation inevitably comes to focus more and more directly on the state. Here the needs of the giant corporations come into play to shape the forms of state activity, partly in ways described by Galbraith, but even more importantly because the system knows no other way than unlimited violence or threats of violence to control the menace of rival social systems and revolutionary national liberation movements.

Notes:

1. What follows is summarized from "Economic Stagnation and Stagnation of Economics," *Monthly Review*, April 1971.
2. Charles Reich, *The Greening of America* (New York: Random House, 1970).
3. J. A. Schumpeter, *The Theory of Economic Development* (Cambridge: Harvard University Press, 1934).
4. Schumpeter, *Capitalism, Socialism and Democracy*, 3d. ed. (New York: Harper and Row, 1950).
5. J. K. Galbraith, *American Capitalism* (Boston: Houghton Mifflin, 1956).
6. Galbraith, *The Affluent Society* (Boston: Houghton Mifflin, 1969).
7. Galbraith, *The New Industrial State* (Boston: Houghton Mifflin, 1967).

8. I exclude such pre-First World War writers as Hilferding, Rosa Luxemburg, and Lenin, who might better be called the founders of what I here call neo-Marxism. It is precisely the failure of later traditionalists to build on the foundations laid by these writers which is responsible for their sterility as theorists of monopoly capitalism.

9. Michal Kalecki, *Theory of Economic Dynamics* (New York: Monthly Review Press, 1968), p. 18.

10. Josef Steindl, *Maturity and Stagnation in American Capitalism* (Oxford: Oxford University Press, 1952).

11. Karl Marx, *Capital,* ed. Kerr, trans. Moore and Aveling (Chicago: Charles H. Kerr, 1906), Vol. I, pp. 168-70. (All references to *Capital* in this book are to either Vol. I or Vol. II of this edition.)

12. B. S. Minhas, "An International Comparison of Factor Cost and Factor Use," mimeographed (Stanford: Department of Economics, Stanford University, 1960).

13. Oskar Lange, *Papers in Economics and Sociology 1930-1960* (London: Pergamon Press, 1970), p. 7.

14. *Capital,* II, p. 169.

Toward a Critique
of Economics

Orthodox economics takes the existing social system for granted, much as though it were part of the natural order of things. Within this framework it searches for harmonies of interest among individuals, groups, classes, and nations; it investigates tendencies toward equilibrium; and it assumes that change is gradual and nondisruptive. I don't think I need to illustrate or support these propositions beyond reminding you that the foundation of all orthodox economics is general and/or partial equilibrium (the two, far from being incompatible, really imply each other). And as for the point about gradualism, I need only recall that printed on the title page of Alfred Marshall's *magnum opus, Principles of Economics,* is the motto *natura non facit saltum* – nature makes no leaps.

It might perhaps be plausibly argued that equilibrium and gradualism provided a workable axiomatic base for a real social science at a certain time and place—the time being

This is the slightly revised text of a talk given at the New England regional meeting of the Union for Radical Political Economics (URPE) held at MIT, November 1-2, 1969. It also appeared in the January 1970 issue of *Monthly Review.*

roughly the half century before the First World War, and the place being Britain and a few other countries of advanced capitalism. For my part, I do not believe this was true even then. I think economics by the time of what may be called the "marginalist revolution" of the 1870s had already practically ceased to be a science and had become mainly an apologetic ideology. Putting harmony, equilibrium, and gradualism at the center of the stage was dictated not by the scientific requirement of fidelity to reality, but by the bourgeois need to prettify and justify a system which was anything but harmonious, equilibrated, and gradualistic.

It was almost at the same time as the marginalist revolution, when economics (as distinct from classical political economy) was being born as an apologetic ideology, that Karl Marx put forward a radically different and opposed mode of analyzing the dominant economic systems. In place of harmony he put conflict. In place of forces tending toward equilibrium he stressed forces tending to disrupt and transform the status quo. In place of gradualism he found qualitative discontinuity. *Natura facit salta* could well have been imprinted on the title page of *Das Kapital.*

It seems to me that from a scientific point of view the question of choosing between these two approaches—the orthodox or the Marxian—can be answered quite simply. Which more accurately reflects the fundamental characteristics of the social reality which is under analysis? I have already indicated my own view that orthodox economics does not reflect that reality but rather serves as an apologetic rationalization for it. Similarly it seems to me that Marxism *does* reflect capitalist reality. Or, to put the matter in other terms, the world we live in is not one of harmonies of interest, tendencies to equilibrium, and gradual change. Rather, it is a world dominated by conflicts of interest, tendencies to disequilibrium, and recurring breaks in the continuity of development. A would-be science which starts with a false or irrelevant conception of reality cannot yield very significant results, no matter how refined and sophisticated its methods may be. The answers a scientist gets depend, first and foremost, not on the methods he uses but on the questions he asks.

This is of course not to denigrate the importance of methods and techniques of investigation. In the development of science they have probably played as important a role as basic theory. The two are in fact intimately interrelated: theory poses questions, methods are devised to answer them, the answers or lack of answers make more theory necessary, and so on *ad infinitum.*

But the scientific endeavor is really not quite so simple and straightforward as this would suggest. Some of you may be familiar with the little book by Thomas S. Kuhn entitled *The Structure of Scientific Revolutions,*[1] which I think is very helpful in this connection. Kuhn argues that every scientific theory rests on what he calls a paradigm, which I think is very close to what I have been referring to as a conception of reality (or of some aspect of reality). Ptolemaic astronomy, for example, rested on a geocentric conception of the cosmos. The questions any science asks are fundamentally limited and conditioned by its underlying paradigm, which in time thus tends to become a hindrance rather than a stimulus to further advance. When this happens, the science in question enters into a period of crisis. The previously existing consensus among its practitioners crumbles. What is now needed is a new paradigm or, in my terminology, a new conception of reality which will once again form the basis for advance. This is often provided, as Kuhn shows in a most interesting way, by outsiders, i.e., men coming to the science from some other field where they have never learned to accept and venerate the conventional wisdom of the science with whose problems they are now concerning themselves. Moreover, as a rule the older scientists are unable to free themselves from their training and preconceptions, while the younger ones find it much easier to accept the new approaches. Gradually a new paradigm emerges and once again provides the basis for theoretical advance and for the unity of the science. In the new phase, what Kuhn calls "normal science" becomes the order of the day, normal science being the posing and answering of the questions which are explicitly or implicitly allowed by the new paradigm or conception of reality.

In Kuhn's view, then, scientific advance takes place not in a straight-line, cumulative manner, starting from small beginnings and building up step-by-step and brick-by-brick to the imposing scientific edifices of today. This, incidentally, is the false idea which not only the lay public but the scientists themselves have of the process of scientific advance, a fact which Kuhn attributes in large part to the role of textbooks in the training of scientists. There are also other reasons of course, among which I would rate as very important the tendency of scientists, in common with other bourgeois thinkers, to view all of history, and not only the history of science, in an undialectical way. The pattern of scientific advance, in Kuhn's view, is rather through the exhaustion and breakdown of paradigms, leading in sequence to crisis, revolution via the construction of a new paradigm, and advance through normal science until a new period of breakdown and crisis is reached.

It would be interesting, and very likely fruitful, to try to apply this schema to the interpretation of the history of the social sciences. But certain obvious complications come to mind. For one thing it is clear that in the social sciences a paradigm can break down not only for what may be called internal reasons—i.e., the exhaustion of the questions it permits to be asked—but also because the social reality which the paradigm reflects undergoes fundamental changes. The crisis of Ptolemaic astronomy did not arise from any change in the functioning of the heavenly bodies, but rather because the geocentric paradigm became increasingly unsatisfactory as a basis for explaining observed phenomena. In the case of social science a new dimension is added: not only the observation of phenomena but the phenomena themselves are subject to change.

Another complicating factor is that the social world involves the *interests* of individuals, groups, classes, nations, in a way that is obviously not the case with the natural world. The resistance to the abandonment of old paradigms and the adoption of new ones is therefore much more complicated and is likely to be much more stubborn in the social sciences than in the natural sciences. I believe it could be shown that one consequence of this is that revolutions in the social sciences are always associated in one way or another with political and social revolutions.

Let us now turn to a consideration of the case of orthodox economics. Here it seems to me that the underlying paradigm, along with the normal science to which it gives rise, can and should be subjected to critical attack on several grounds. As I have already suggested, this paradigm takes the existing social order for granted, which means that it assumes, implicitly if not explicitly, that the capitalist system is permanent. Further, it assumes that within this system (a) the interests of individuals, groups, and classes are harmonious (or, if not harmonious, at least reconcilable); (b) tendencies to equilibrium exist and assert themselves in the long run; and (c) change is and will continue to be gradual and adaptive.

One line of attack would be that this paradigm is about a century old and that most of the basic questions it allows to be asked have long since been posed and explored by the great economists of the first and second generations—men like Menger, Wieser, Böhm-Bawerk, and Wicksell in one tradition; Walras, Pareto, and the early mathematical economists in another tradition; and Marshall, Pigou, and Keynes in still another. (The list is of course intended to be illustrative rather than exhaustive.) More recent orthodox economics, remaining within the same fundamental limits, has therefore tended, so to speak, to yield diminishing returns. It has concerned itself with smaller and decreasingly significant questions, even judging magnitude and significance by its own standards. To compensate for this trivialization of content, it has paid increasing attention to elaborating and refining its techniques. The consequence is that today we often find a truly stupefying gap between the questions posed and the techniques employed to answer them. Let me cite, only partly for your amusement, one of the more extreme examples of this disparity that I happen to have run across:

> Given a set of economic agents and a set of coalitions, a non-empty family of subsets of the first set closed under the formation of countable unions and complements, an allocation is a countable additive function from the set of coalitions to the closed positive orthant of the commodity space. To describe preferences in this context, one can either introduce a positive, finite real measure defined on the set of coalitions and specify, for each agent, a relation of preference-or-indifference on the closed positive orthant of the commodity space, or specify, for each coalition, a relation of the preference-or-indifference on the set of allocations. This article studies the extent to which these two approaches are equivalent.[2]

You will doubtless be glad to know that in his search for an answer to this momentous question the author enjoyed the support of the National Science Foundation and the Office of Naval Research.

But a much more fundamental line of attack on orthodox economics proceeds from the proposition that, whatever relative validity its underlying paradigm may have had a hundred years ago has largely disappeared as a result of intervening changes in the global structure and functioning of the capitalist system. Conflicts of interest, disruptive forces, abrupt and often violent change—these are clearly the *dominant* characteristics of capitalism on a worldwide scale today. But they are outside the self-imposed limits of orthodox economics, which is therefore condemned to increasing irrelevance and impotence.

Before I turn in conclusion to the state of Marxian economics, let me add that what I have been saying applies to economics considered as a social science, as the modern successor to classical political economy, whose task is to comprehend the *modus operandi* of the socioeconomic system. I quite realize that a great deal of what is actually taught in economics departments today and is *called* economics is something entirely different. It seeks not to understand a certain aspect of reality but rather to devise ways and means of manipulating *given* institutions and variables to achieve results which for one reason or another are considered desirable. How should a corporation allocate its resources to obtain maximum profits? How should a government department weigh costs and benefits in making its decisions? How can a centrally planned society achieve a distribution of goods and services and a rate of growth in conformity with the directives of its political authorities?

Naturally, I have no objection to asking and trying to answer questions of this kind, and I suppose it is no great matter that the work is carried out in economics departments (as well as in business schools, departments of public administration, and the like). What I do object to is calling this sort of thing "science." It is no more social science than engineering is physical science. The analogy may not be perfect, but I do not think it is basically misleading either. I will only add that I think a great deal of this social "engineering" is vitiated by taking its assumptions about how economic entities and institutions work from what I consider faulty social science. Here the analogy certainly does work: engineering isn't physics or chemistry, but its success depends on making use of the scientific laws of physics and chemistry. Social engineering is in the same state of dependence, and this explains why much of it is beside the point or worse. Try, for example, to prescribe a solution for a problem involving irreconcilable conflicts of interest on the assumption of underlying harmony. This, as it happens, is being done all the time in the United States today—with respect to such problems as the racial and urban crises, relations between the advanced and underdeveloped countries, and many others.

Now in conclusion a few words about Marxian economics. Here the underlying paradigm stressing conflict, disequilibrium, and discontinuity is also about a hundred years old. Since the knowledge which it yields is totally critical of the existing society, it was naturally unacceptable to the beneficiaries of that social order—in the first instance the propertied classes which are also the possessors of political power. Marxian economics was therefore banned from all the established institutions of society such as government, schools, colleges, and universities. As a result it became the social science of the individuals and classes in revolt against the existing social order. Three points need to be emphasized here:

(1) The class character of Marxian economics in no way calls into question or impugns its scientific validity. That depends entirely on its ability to explain reality. And in this respect it seems clear, to me at any rate, that the record of Marxian economics is far better than that of orthodox economics.

(2) But it also seems to me that the record is not anywhere

near as good as it could have been. There are probably several reasons for this, only one of which will be mentioned here. This is that the practice of "normal science" within the framework of the Marxian paradigm has from the beginning been extremely difficult. Excluded from universities and research institutes, Marxian economists have generally lacked the facilities, the time, and the congenial environment available to other scientists. Most of them have had to make their living at other jobs, often in the nerve-racking and fatiguing area of political activism. In these circumstances what is perhaps remarkable is that so much rather than so little has been accomplished.

(3) But why, it may be asked, have not the revolutions of the twentieth century, mostly espousing Marxism as their official ideology, not resulted in a flowering of Marxian economics (and other social sciences)? Here, I think, we meet a paradox which, however, can be explained by a Marxian analysis. Revolutionary regimes so far this century have come to power in relatively backward countries and have been largely preoccupied with retaining power against internal and external enemies. In these circumstances, their attitudes toward Marxism as a social science have been ambivalent for the simple reason that it is, or is always likely to become, critical of the new social order. It follows that under revolutionary regimes, as under the previous capitalist regimes, for Marxists the practice of normal science has been difficult and often practically impossible.

I do not want to end these remarks on such a negative note. Despite all the hindrances and difficulties, I think Marxian economics has indeed made notable progress and produced important contributions to our understanding of today's world. Let me cite just one area in which I think its superiority over orthodox economics is obvious and overwhelming—in explaining what has often been called the most important problem of the twentieth century, the growing gap between a handful of advanced capitalist countries and the so-called Third World.

Orthodox economics has nothing useful to say on this subject—largely, I would argue, because it is ruled out by the underlying paradigm. And the prescriptions of orthodox economics for overcoming the gap have been proving their impotence for many years now.

For Marxian economics, on the other hand, the explanation, if not simple, is at least perfectly clear in its main outlines. This explanation can be put schematically as follows:

(1) From the beginning, the development of today's advanced capitalist countries has been based on subjugation and exploitation of Third World countries. The latter's pre-existing societies were largely destroyed, and they were then reorganized to serve the purposes of the conquerors. The wealth transferred to the advanced countries was one of their chief sources of capital accumulation.

(2) The relations established between the two groups of countries—trade, investment, and more recently so-called aid—have been such as to promote development in the one and underdevelopment in the other.

(3) There is therefore nothing at all mysterious about either the gap or its widening. Both are the inevitable consequence of the global structure of the capitalist system.

(4) It follows that the situation can be changed and real development can take place in the Third World only if the existing pattern of relations is decisively broken. The countries of the Third World must secure control over their own economic surplus and use it not for the enrichment of others but for their own development and their own people. This means thoroughgoing revolution to overthrow imperialism and its local allies and agents.

Marxian economists still have a tremendous amount of

work to do to explain and elucidate the many complex facets of this global process. But I suggest that in the work of such outstanding Marxists as the late Paul Baran and Andre Gunder Frank great strides have been made in recent years, and that large numbers of dedicated young social scientists, not least in the Third World itself, are not only following in their footsteps but pushing on to new frontiers.

Can anything remotely comparable be said of the contribution of orthodox economists? I think the answer is obvious. And the thought I would leave you with is that the fault lies not in any lack of talent or dedication on the part of the practitioners of orthodox economics, but rather in the fundamental falsity of the conception of reality which underlies all their theoretical and empirical work.

Notes:

1. Thomas S. Kuhn, *The Structure of Scientific Revolutions* (Chicago: University of Chicago Press, Phoenix Books, 1962).
2. Gerard Debreu, "Preference Functions on Measure Spaces of Economic Agents," mimeographed (Berkeley: Center for Research in Management Science, University of California, January 1966).

Theories of the New Capitalism

Few would quarrel with the proposition that capitalism is a highly dynamic, rapidly changing social order. Marx and Engels put the point at its strongest when they wrote in the *Communist Manifesto:*

> The bourgeoisie cannot exist without constantly revolutionizing the instruments of production, and thereby the relations of production, and with them the whole relations of society. . . . Constant revolutionizing of production, uninterrupted disturbance of all social conditions, everlasting uncertainty and agitation distinguish the bourgeois epoch from all earlier ones. All fixed, fast frozen relations . . . are swept away, all new-formed ones become antiquated before they can ossify.

It would be easy to argue on these grounds that capitalism is always and inevitably a "new capitalism" in relation to what went before, and indeed there is a sense in which this is unquestionably true and important. But clearly it is not what

This article appeared in the July/August 1959 issue of *Monthly Review*.

is meant by all those people, representing many shades of opinion, who apply the name "new capitalism" (or some label with a similar connotation) to the present socioeconomic system of the United States. They mean not just that the system continues, as in the past, to evolve in various unspecified ways but rather that in recent years it has undergone a number of specific changes which have decisively altered its mode of functioning.

If we try to pin down just what these specific changes are, however, we find less agreement and even not a little confusion. Haig Babian, editor of *Challenge* magazine, published by New York University's Institute of Economic Affairs, has the following to say in an editorial introducing a special issue (October 1958) devoted entirely to the "new capitalism":

> It would be fitting to present in this editorial some clear and concise definition of what we mean by the term New Capitalism, but I must admit that such a clear and concise definition escapes me. Nevertheless, I feel no less incapable in this respect than the vast majority of my fellow citizens. It is much easier to say what the New Capitalism is not. It is not the classical capitalism so well studied in the past and so imperfectly practiced today. What it is remains to be seen.

The reader who expects clarification from the twelve essays that follow Babian's introduction is likely to be disappointed, however. Most of them are by eminent economists and political scientists, and a number are of considerably more than passing interest. But they yield no agreement on the nature of the new capitalism, and some of the authors even shy rather conspicuously away from using the term.

Is all this to be taken as evidence that the new capitalism is an illusion? Not necessarily. The mere absence of a "clear and concise definition" of something doesn't prove that it doesn't exist, and in this case the remarkably widespread belief in the reality of some sort of new capitalism is at least *prima facie* evidence that it does exist. But the question remains: what is it?

One way to approach this question is via a critical analysis of the actual content of some of the better-known recent literature dealing with capitalism. I have tried to keep track of this literature with reasonable care, and what follows is an attempt to pick out the themes which stand out by reason of frequent repetition or particular emphasis or both. Since any systematic survey of sources—not to mention quotation of texts—is out of the question in a brief essay, I have cited works and authors rather to enliven the exposition than to prove points. A short list of what seem to me to be the more important and representative works (including all those cited) will be found at the end of the essay. Rather than burden the text with titles, I refer to these works by numbers enclosed in brackets.

Breakdown of the Classical Model

All the writers on the new capitalism agree on one thing: the classical model of a freely competitive and self-adjusting economy no longer reflects the essentials of capitalist reality. In this model, all prices (including wages, rents, and rates of interest) were determined by the bids and offers of innumerable buyers and sellers each too small to affect the outcome by his own action. The interplay of supply, demand, and price was supposed to ensure that commodities would be produced in the right proportions, that productive resources would be correctly allocated and efficiently utilized, and that factors of production would be rewarded in accordance with their productivity. In addition, given competitive pricing, a slump could be no more than a temporary phenomenon since a general excess of supply must necessarily depress prices to the point where demand would once again clear the market.

This idyllic picture does not apply to the new capitalism. The decisive capitalist enterprise is no longer the small individually owned firm but the giant corporation in which management is separated from ownership and which typically controls so large a share of the market that it can, within fairly wide limits, set its own prices. As we shall see presently, the theorists of the new capitalism are far from unanimous about how an economy dominated by big corporations does function, but at any rate they are fully agreed that it does not and could not function in the manner of the classical model. Perhaps the clearest and most concise spelling out of the reasons why the classical model is not applicable in the new circumstances is to be found in Galbraith [9], especially Chapter IV. Strachey [16] also gives a good account of the matter.

The Corporate Economy

There are at least four distinguishable, though in certain respects overlapping, views about how an economic model dominated by a relatively few big corporations should be expected to function. I shall describe them under the following somewhat arbitrary headings: (a) The "New" Competition, (b) Countervailing Power, (c) The Corporate Soul, and (d) Unchecked Oligopoly.

The "New" Competition. According to some writers, notably the editors of *Fortune* [8] and David Lilienthal [12], the corporate economy generates a new kind of competition which works not only as well as but actually much better than the old kind. Price competition, to be sure, is out or at any rate relegated to a relatively minor role. In its place we have, first, competition in service and quality, and second, competition in innovation (development of both new products and new methods of production). The latter is supposed to be the more important of the two kinds of competition, and indeed is said to be responsible for lending to the new capitalism an enormously dynamic and progressive character with an unlimited growth potential. Under these circumstances, all the old depression-born fears of maturity or stagnation are quite groundless: the problem of the new corporate capitalism is not a shortage of investment outlets but lack of enough investment-seeking funds to realize its full possibilities. These ideas about the new competition and its wondrous promise for the future, incidentally, closely parallel and perhaps to a certain extent reflect theoretical currents in the economics profession. Schumpeter [15] preached the technological progressiveness of the big corporation long before it became a popular theme, while J. M. Clark [5] and E. S. Mason [14] took the lead in developing a notion of "workable competition" which they hoped would be as economically efficacious as the "free," "pure," or "perfect" competition of the past.

Countervailing Power. This theory is the special product of J. K. Galbraith [9]. It maintains that wherever dangerous power develops on one side of a market, there will grow up on the other side (either spontaneously as in the case of chain stores or mail-order houses, or with government assistance as in the case of agriculture and labor) a countervailing power which holds the original power in check. Thus despite the growth of potentially overweening monopolies (or oligopolies), the new capitalism develops a new self-adjusting mechanism which takes the place of the old competition. In a review of Galbraith's *American Capitalism,* Joan Robinson wittily and aptly characterized this theory as an effort at "re-bunking laissez faire."

The Corporate Soul. The idea that the managers of the modern corporation no longer seek to maximize profits but in effect act as trustees of the whole community goes back to the well-known work of Berle and Means published in 1932 [3]. Since then it has been developed by the same authors, notably Berle [2], and has been taken up by many others, including professional economists (see especially Kaysen [11] for a clear, concise statement). In place of the old-fashioned "soulless" corporation we now have the modern "soulful" corporation seeking to do its best not only for stockholders but also for workers, customers, suppliers, and the general public. A system dominated by soulful corporations is supposed to operate very differently from the old profit-oriented capitalism. To listen to Berle, indeed, one gets the impression that modern corporations have instituted a regime of economic planning, in principle very similar to that in force in the Soviet Union. Such a system is naturally not threatened by the inequalities and instabilities which used to beset the old capitalism.

Unchecked Oligopoly. Almost alone among the theorists of the new capitalism (he usually calls it "last stage capitalism"), John Strachey [16] holds that *on purely economic grounds* the oligopolistic system of large corporations tends to develop *greater instability* and *more extreme inequality* than the competitive capitalist order. This is because Strachey believes, in opposition to Berle et al., that the big corporation is still profit oriented, and its great market power enables it to realize much larger profits than its competitive ancestors could hope to earn. Large profits in turn are the source of both instability and inequality (this follows from a style of reasoning which is common to both Keynesism and Marxism, which are judiciously mixed in Strachey's economic theory). If the new capitalism nevertheless does not break down, but on the contrary functions with greater justice and efficiency than the old, the reason, in Strachey's view, must be sought not in the economics of the system but in its politics. And this brings us to a subject which it will be preferable to treat under a separate heading, namely, the role of the state in the new capitalism.

Role of the State in the New Capitalism

All of the theories of a new capitalism assign to the state both a different role and a larger role than the one it was supposed to perform in the classical and Marxian theories of the *modus operandi* of capitalist society. Nevertheless, there are differences of interpretation and emphasis.

John Strachey, as we have seen, finds that recent economic developments have tended to worsen the performance of capitalism but believes that these have been more than compensated in the political sphere. The active force here he sees as "democracy," which operates in many ways (through trade unions and labor-based political parties of course, but also through conservative parties) and makes use of the most varied means to achieve its goals of full employment, equality, social welfare, and the like. The struggle between democracy and the inherent tendencies of corporate capitalism is unremitting and will finally end only with the suppression of democracy or the transformation of the system into full-fledged socialism. In the meantime, however, and as a by-product of this struggle, capitalism works much better than it used to. This, according to Strachey, is the secret of the latest—and what he takes to be the last—phase of capitalism.

An equally sophisticated but somewhat different theory has been put forward by the governing party of Yugoslavia [17]. According to this view, the decisive factor is not so much "democracy" as the state bureaucracy which is supposed to achieve a considerable degree of independence in the most advanced capitalist countries. This relatively independent governing stratum is able to carry out reforms and put into practice policies which modify the workings of the traditional capitalist system. Looked at in longer perspective, this state of affairs is seen by the Yugoslav theorists as transitional, already partially transcending capitalism and establishing foundations for socialist growth in the future.

American writers on the new capitalism also stress the role of the state, but without feeling the need of any particular political theory to explain or justify it. The pragmatic experiments of the New Deal, the promptings of Keynesian theory, the compulsions of war and cold war—these are generally taken to have been the stages and factors which have propelled the state into a new economic role. But whatever their ideas about the causative factors at work, these American writers are in close agreement about two points: first, that the new role of the state is permanent and can now be treated as an integral feature of the system; and second, that the ability of the state to prevent a serious depression can be taken for granted—and this regardless of what happens in the field of armaments. Beyond this area of agreement there are, of course, differences about how much credit for the relatively favorable performance of capitalism in recent years should go to the state, and also about how much and what kinds of action the state will be called upon to take in the future. The "managerial" writers like Berle and the editors of *Fortune* generally play down the importance of the state, while "New Dealers" like Galbraith play it up and believe that the role of the state will inevitably continue to expand in the future. In practice, it may be noted, the position of the latter group is almost indistinguishable from the seemingly more radical socialist position of Strachey, a position which incidentally is shared by most articulate European social democrats.

Doubts and Criticisms

All the ideas and theories which have been surveyed have, naturally enough, been subjected to scrutiny and criticism, often from within the camp of believers in a new capitalism and perhaps even more frequently from more orthodox or skeptical sections of the economics profession. Here we shall have to be content with a desperately brief notice of some of the more important doubts and criticisms.

From the economics profession, the most devastating critique has been that of E. S. Mason [13], professor of economics at Harvard and formerly dean of the Harvard Graduate School of Public Administration. Mason does a workmanlike job of showing that the whole range of "managerial" thought—and in this classification he includes what we have subsumed under the headings of new competition, countervailing power, and the soulful corporation—is, to put the point bluntly, superficial and hardly to be taken seriously. Of the exponents of the new competition he says that they "have hardly begun to grapple with the real problems implicit in their view of the structure and functioning of industrial markets." And he might have added that if and when they do grapple with these problems (a most unlikely contingency, by the way) they will find that even the most vigorous forms of non-price competition can in no way alter the logic of John Strachey's argument that oligopoly, left to itself, means higher profits, and higher profits mean more instability and greater inequality. With regard to countervailing power, Mason says: "The 'countervailers' have never been able to explain why countervailance does not lead merely to a sharing of monopoly profits at the expense of the rest of the economy." One is reminded of the witty remark of an early reviewer of Galbraith's book [9] to the effect that possibly some of the alleged countervailing powers may veil more power than they counter.[1] And of the alleged beneficence of soulful corporations, Mason has the following to say:

> Assume an economy composed of a few hundred large corporations, each enjoying substantial market power and all directed by managements with a "conscience." Each management wants to do the best it can for labor, customers, suppliers, and owners. How do prices get determined in such an economy? How are factors remunerated, and what relation is there between remuneration and performance? What is the mechanism, if any, that assures effective resource use, and how can corporate managements "do right by" labor, suppliers, customers, and owners while simultaneously serving the public interests? ... I can find no reasoned answer in the managerial literature.

The answer of course is that if a few hundred sovereign corporations all took it upon themselves to plan in the public interest, the result would be not a new capitalism but simple chaos. Fortunately for capitalism, however, this at any rate is not one of its more pressing problems. Professor James Earley [7], of the University of Wisconsin, has shown on the basis of empirical studies such as none of the managerialists has ever bothered to carry out that the modern giant corporation is more, not less, profit oriented than its small-scale predecessor.

Mason's riddling—and in part ridiculing—of managerial theories is the more impressive in that it was never any part of his purpose to cast disparagement on capitalism, old or new. On the contrary, his interest in these theories stemmed from a belief that a new rationalization and justification of capitalism (he calls it an "apologetic") is needed to take the place of the now outdated classical theory based on the assumption of free competition. Mason's examination of the various versions of managerialism—and in his usage this takes in most of what we have included under the heading of theories of the new capitalism—shows, however, that nothing is to be expected from this quarter. "The attack on the capitalist apologetic of the nineteenth century has been successful," he concludes, "but a satisfactory contemporary apologetic is still to be created." And he adds that he suspects that "the psychologists, the sociologists, and, possibly, the political scientists" will have more to contribute to it than will the economists. The article ends on a worried note: "It is high time they were called to their job."

Mason is certainly right about the impotence of economics before this task. The entire logic of economic theory points to the conclusion reached by John Strachey: the immanent tendency of an oligopolistic economy of giant corporations is toward ever more inequality and ever greater instability. This does not negate the argument in favor of such an economy (as opposed to small-scale competitive capitalism) on the grounds of superior technological progressiveness. Manifestly, in an age of science and organized research the big corporation *is* much better equipped to innovate than the individual entrepreneur.[2] There is, however, no reason to equate rapid technological advance with unlimited investment opportunity. A high rate of technological progress can be financed from depreciation allowances—that is to say, with no net investment at all—and to the extent that new technologies are both labor-saving and capital-saving they may just as well exacerbate as ameliorate the problem of providing investment outlets for the swelling tide of profits which the big corporations tend to generate. Whatever satisfaction one may derive from the technological performance of the big corporations, clearly there is no ground for supposing that an economy dominated by them, if left to itself, would function any more satisfactorily than the old-fashioned capitalism it replaced.

This brings us back again to the role of the state. What are we to say about Strachey's theory that "democracy" makes all the difference to the functioning of capitalism? If one were to confine one's attention to postwar Britain and a few of the smaller Western European countries, one could perhaps make out a case for this theory, but as a generalization there is little to be said in its favor. The first large-scale experiment in the Welfare State was carried out by Imperial Germany under Bismarck, hardly a model of democracy. And the first successful, albeit, unconscious, application of Keynesian economics was the work of Hitler. At the very same time, the United States under the New Deal was in what may have been the most democratic phase of the country's entire history—and continued to suffer from mass unemployment on an unprecedented scale. In the face of facts such as these, it is hard to take seriously a theory which attributes a decisive change in the functioning of capitalism to democratically motivated (or generated) state intervention.

The Yugoslav theory of the independent state bureaucracy is, if anything, even less convincing. So far as the United States is concerned, for example, there has probably never been a time when the whole state apparatus has been more securely in the control of Big Business than during the 1950s.

Not that all those writers are wrong who stress the increased economic role of the state under capitalism. That such an increase has indeed taken place, and that it has had its effect on the functioning of the system—these are matters of common observation which no one could deny. But this appears to be a long-term trend which has operated under democratic and dictatorial governments alike and which has little or nothing to do with the character of the state bureaucracy. How it is related to capitalism and in just what sense it may be said to have produced a *new* capitalism are questions which none of the theories we have been surveying seriously tackles, let alone successfully answers. The truth is that these theories, purged of their errors and illogicalities, boil down to a few simple propositions about the increased economic importance of the state and the absence of sharp or prolonged depressions in the period since the Second World War. In this form the theories are quite unexceptionable—and equally unenlightening.

Concluding Remarks

Let me conclude with a few suggestions as to what it seems to me ought to be the Marxist view of the issues raised in this article.

First, whether one calls present-day capitalism "new" or "last stage" or what have you is not a matter of great importance. But it *is* important to recognize—and not to lose sight of—the fact that in some respects the system has worked better in recent years than it used to. This is particularly true with respect to the severity (though not the frequency) of depressions.

Second, the "new capitalism" theories are right to stress that the old-fashioned competitive, self-adjusting model is no longer applicable. They are also right to insist on the *dominant* role of giant monopolistic (or oligopolistic) corporations.

Third, John Strachey is right to argue that the immanent tendency of a capitalist economy dominated by giant corporations is toward more, not less, inequality and instability. In the absence of counteracting forces, such an economy tends to bog down in chronic and self-destructive depression—as indeed the American economy did in the years after 1929.

Fourth, the system itself—and not "democracy" or an independent state bureaucracy—generates counteracting forces. They can all be subsumed under the general heading of waste. Some of the waste is private—salesmanship, fins, planned obsolescence, and so on and so forth. Private waste, however, is insufficient and the government is called upon to help. Because of democracy and such independence as the state bureaucracy may possess, there is a tendency for the state to embark on welfare and other types of useful projects, but the vested interests imbedded in the system set up the most powerful kind of blockages, and (so far at any rate) the only type of government activity that has been sustained on an adequate scale is the purely wasteful one of war preparations. *It should never be forgotten that quantitatively the only really new feature of post-Second World War capitalism is the vastly increased size of the arms budget. All other government spending is about the same percentage of the Gross National Product as in 1929.* Further, there is no reason except wishful thinking for believing if the arms budget were reduced to the proportions of the 1930s that the the economy would not once again revert to the condition of the 1930s.

Finally, it should be no part of the Marxist view that all this is inevitable and must remain unchanged until the day of the socialist revolution. Perhaps, in a world going socialist, a determined democratic movement in the advanced capitalist countries—or at least in some of them—can make the welfare state a real substitute for the warfare state. But it hasn't happened yet.

Notes:

1. C. L. Christenson in the *Journal of Political Economy,* June 1952, pp. 275-76.
2. But see Philip Morrison, "The Innovation Industry," *Monthly Review,* July/August 1959, pp. 103-10.

Selected Works Relevant to the "New Capitalism"

1. Paul A. Baran, "Reflections on Underconsumption," in *The Longer View* (New York: Monthly Review Press, 1970), pp. 185-202.
2. A. A. Berle, Jr., *The 20th Century Capitalist Revolution* (New York: Harcourt, Brace and World, 1954).
3. A. A. Berle, Jr. and Gardner C. Means, *The Modern Corporation and Private Property,* rev. ed. (New York: Harcourt, Brace, Jovanovich, 1969).
4. James Burnham, *The Managerial Revolution* (Bloomington: Indiana University Press, 1960).
5. J. M. Clark, "Toward a Concept of Workable Competition," *American Economic Review,* June 1940.
6. C. A. R. Crosland, *The Future of Socialism* (New York: Schocken Books, 1963).
7. James Earley, in *Papers and Proceedings of the American Economic Association 1956,* May 1957.
8. Editors of *Fortune, U.S.A.: The Permanent Revolution* (New York: Prentice-Hall, 1951).
9. Galbraith, *American Capitalism.*
10. Galbraith, *The Affluent Society.*
11. Carl Kaysen, "The Social Significance of the Modern Corporation," in *Papers and Proceedings of the American Economic Association 1956,* May 1957.
12. David Lilienthal, *Big Business: A New Era* (New York: Harper Bros., 1953).
13. E. S. Mason, "The Apologetics of 'Managerialism,' " *The Journal of Business,* January 1958.
14. Mason in "The Antitrust Laws: A Symposium," ed. Dexter M. Keezer, *American Economic Review,* June 1949.
15. Schumpeter, *Capitalism, Socialism and Democracy.*
16. John Strachey, *Contemporary Capitalism* (New York: Random House, 1956).
17. *Yugoslavia's Way: Program of the League of Communists of Yugoslavia* (1958).

Keynesian Economics: The First Quarter Century

Apart from minor matters of formulation and emphasis, I am prepared to stand by what I wrote a decade and a half ago about Keynes and Keynesian economics.[1] In particular, I still believe that his greatest achievements were freeing economics from the tyranny of Say's Law and exploding the myth of capitalism as a self-adjusting system which reconciles private and public interests.

In this connection, however, I would like to amend what I wrote earlier, not because the amendment is of any particular importance in itself but because it provides a logical introduction to the remarks which constitute the substance of what follows.

Starting from the rejection of Say's Law, I wrote, Keynes "was able to go on to a penetrating analysis of the capitalist

Reprinted from Robert Lekachman, ed., *Keynes' General Theory: Reports on Three Decades,* rev. ed. (New York: St. Martin's Press, 1968), by permission of St. Martin's Press, Macmillan London and Basingstoke, and the Royal Economic Society, London; originally written in 1963 for the first edition of the Lekachman volume.

economy which shows that depression and unemployment, far from being impossible, are the norms to which the economy tends." This now seems to me to be a misleading statement of the case. Keynes in fact did not "show" anything of the kind, at least not in the sense of furnishing a logical, consistent, and convincing set of reasons why it should be so. He *believed* that the inducement to invest was, so to speak, naturally weak and that the structure of the system was such that a weak inducement to invest would result in depression and unemployment. His analysis was focused on this structure, and he gave reasons (essentially downward rigidity of wage and interest rates) why it could not generate full employment in the absence of a strong inducement to invest. But he had very little indeed to say about why the inducement to invest should be chronically weak, and this, after all, lies at the heart of the matter.

It is not hard to infer from remarks scattered here and there throughout the *General Theory* that Keynes believed that at any given time the demand for capital is narrowly limited and hence that the maintenance of a strong inducement to invest depends almost entirely on what are often called exogenous factors. Perhaps the most explicit statement of this thesis occurs on page 307:

> During the nineteenth century, the growth of population and of invention, the opening up of new lands, the state of confidence and the frequency of war over the average of (say) each decade seem to have been sufficient, taken in conjunction with the propensity to consume, to establish a schedule of the marginal efficiency of capital which allowed a reasonably satisfactory average level of employment to be compatible with a rate of interest high enough to be psychologically acceptable to wealth-owners.

So much for the nineteenth century. What of the twentieth? On the following page, we read: "To-day and presumably for the future the schedule of the marginal efficiency of capital is, for a variety of reasons, much lower than it was in the nineteenth century." One might expect to find this followed by a discussion of the "variety of reasons," but if so one would be disappointed. Keynes turns immediately to the downward stickiness of the rate of interest and forgets all about the flagging marginal efficiency of capital. Nor does a careful reading of the rest of the *General Theory*, or of his other writings either for that matter, yield any but casual and often peripheral remarks bearing on the subject.[2]

About all one can say, then, is that Keynes seems to have been of the opinion that "the growth of population and of invention, the opening up of new lands, the state of confidence and the frequency of war," taken all together, had lost much of their efficacy as stimulants to the demand for capital. This is not much of a theory, and it is even less impressive when one looks, in even the most superficial way, at the historical record. On a world scale, population growth has speeded up rather than the reverse, and in an economic sense there has been no lack of underdeveloped lands. Nor can one very well complain about a shortage of wars during the twentieth century. That leaves the state of confidence, which is obviously a reflection rather than a cause of the underlying situation. The truth would seem to be that the "vision" of capitalism as a system always in imminent danger of falling into a state of stagnation—a vision which permeates, and in a sense even dominates, the *General Theory*—is based more on intuition and generalizing from British experience of the 1920s and early 1930s than on any serious analysis of the factors affecting the inducement to invest.

Among Keynes' followers, only Hansen undertook to develop a *theory* of the tendency to stagnation. This theory turns out, however, to be little more than an elaboration, in terms of U.S. experience, of Keynes' casual remark quoted above. According to Hansen, the stagnation of the 1930s was caused by declining investment opportunities uncompensated by a corresponding decline in the propensity to save. Declining investment opportunities, in turn, he traced to a slowing up of the rate of population growth, the closing of the frontier, and (more tentatively) an increasing capital-saving bias in the newer technologies. This is not the place for a detailed discussion of these various factors and their relation to the inducement to invest: I will only say that while I found Hansen's theory persuasive when it was first put forward, subsequent criticisms and developments seem to me to have convincingly refuted it. It is the growth of purchasing power, not population, that counts, and the relationship between the two is anything but clear. Further, the experience of the war and immediate postwar periods suggests that population is, economically speaking, more a dependent than an independent variable. No one has ever succeeded in demonstrating a relation between the closing of the frontier in the 1890s (or whenever it is supposed to have been closed) and the demand for capital in the 1930s. And it is anyone's guess whether either the character of technolog-ical change or its effect on investment is of the kind postulated in Hansen's theory.

Thus neither Keynes nor his followers really provided an explanation of the stagnation of the 1930s. Their whole analysis was directed to showing that *if* the inducement to invest is weak, the capitalist system, left to itself, will stagnate. But they had nothing very enlightening to say about *why* it should be (or remain) weaker than it had been in the past. Nor were other attempts at an explanation any more successful. Perhaps the most elaborate was that of Schum-peter who saw the allegedly anticapitalist politics of the New Deal as the villain of the piece, a view that was devastatingly refuted by one of Schumpeter's own students and warmest admirers.[3] It is, I believe, no exaggeration to say that while Keynes and his followers had done a lot to clarify the mechanics of the capitalist system, neither they nor anyone else in the economics profession made any real progress in solving the mystery of the extraordinary depth and duration of the Great Depression. When the Second World War came along, they gave up trying.

And yet the problem was still there and still crying out for a solution. Furthermore, clues to a promising line of attack were not lacking. Several years before the publication of the *General Theory*, bourgeois social science had effected two complementary and almost simultaneous breakthroughs in the study of capitalism. One, associated with the names of Sraffa, Chamberlin, and Joan Robinson, was a great stride forward in the theory of noncompetitive markets. The other, associated with the names of Berle and Means, was the demonstration of the extent to which the U.S. economy (and, by easy inference, others in a comparable stage of development) was *dominated* by huge corporations that by no stretch of the imagination could be assumed to behave like the entrepreneurs of classical and neoclassical theory. In retrospect, it seems odd that these two developments did not suggest, almost at once, the need for far-reaching revisions in macroeconomic theory, which in all its versions was still based on the assumption of universal competition.

I'm not sure why this didn't happen. Perhaps the explanation is the strong grip of a deeply rooted intellectual tradition, essentially the same explanation that Keynes offered for the continued acceptance of Say's Law long after its contradiction by everyday experience should have been obvious to everyone.[4] In any case, it didn't happen, not even in Cambridge where the noncompetitive market theories originated. In particular, the *General Theory* shows absolutely no trace of "monopolistic thinking," and its tremendous impact and prestige doubtless served as an additional bulwark of the traditional assumption of universal competition. My own opinion now, many years later, is that it was the stubborn commitment to this assumption—the refusal to contemplate, let alone work out the implications of, the possibility that monopoly (or oligopoly) had become the norm—which accounts for the failure of Keynesians and non-Keynesians alike to make any progress in developing a satisfactory theory of what happened during the 1930s.

To be sure, there was one notable exception. Michal Kalecki not only "discovered the *General Theory* independently,"[5] he was also the first to include what he called the "degree of monopoly" in his overall model of the economy. Kalecki showed that an increase in the degree of monopoly will cause a relative shift from wages to profits and hence will act to slow down the long-run rate of increase in output.[6] He did not, however, stress the point, apparently considering it to be of relatively minor importance.[7]

It was left for Josef Steindl, an Austrian economist who spent the Hitler period at Oxford, to follow up Kalecki's tentative lead by constructing a consistent theory of stagnation around the monopolization process which had been so dramatically documented by Berle and Means. There is, of course, plenty of room for agreement or disagreement with Steindl, but at any rate one would have expected that his work, *Maturity and Stagnation in American Capitalism,* would have been greeted with intense interest as (a) the first full-scale welding together of the two great theoretical advances of the recent past—the theory of noncompetitive markets on the micro level and the theory of income and employment on the macro level—and (b) the only serious effort since Hansen and Schumpeter to solve the mystery of the thirties. In fact, however, nothing of the sort happened. Steindl's book was greeted with resounding silence; and I would guess that today, ten years after its publication, a majority of the U.S. economics profession doesn't even know of its existence. It seems quite safe to say that in the whole history of economic thought there is not another instance of so important a work being so completely neglected. Only Paul Baran gave it its due, and the Marxist orientation of his *Political Economy of Growth*[8] acted, as always, to insure that this extremely important work would get the same reception from the profession that Steindl's had already received.

Why was Steindl's *Maturity and Stagnation* treated this way? In one sense, the answer is obvious. It was published in 1952, in the middle of the Korean War boom and after more than a decade of almost continuous full or near-full employment. To bourgeois economists, stagnation seemed like ancient history, and they just weren't interested.

But of course this is only the superficial aspect of the matter. What really needs explaining is why economists are so completely dominated by the moment, how it could happen that a problem which had been so hotly debated within the lifetime of all the economists then alive could have been so quickly forgotten, why a serious attempt to advance their own theories should fail to arouse their purely *scientific* interest.

I suggest that the explanation must be sought along two main lines. First, there is the natural aversion of the ideological champions of capitalism to a theory with profoundly disturbing implications for the stability and even viability of the system. This aversion was, of course, nothing new, and it played a big part in determining attitudes toward Keynes and the *General Theory*. But during the 1930s it was impossible to deny or ignore capitalism's troubles. In the early 1950s, it was easy.

Second and more basic, there is the deeply ingrained un- and antihistorical core alike of classical political economy and of neoclassical economics. Advanced capitalism, as it existed in Britain in the nineteenth century and later in a handful of European and North American countries, was and is looked upon as the end product of economic evolution. The focus of economic theory is this system's tendencies to equilibrium (or disequilibrium) and its short-run fluctuations. No genuine trends—in Marxian terminology, no "laws of motion"—are conceded to exist, still less subjected to analysis. Keynes remained strictly within this tradition, the only difference being that he made no effort to dress up capitalist equilibria as ideal or desirable states; and Keynes' followers have also remained within it. Steindl's work, in contrast, is basically an attempt to work out a theory of the evolution of advanced (monopoly) capitalism. As such it is entirely alien to the whole orthodox tradition, and this in spite of the fact that Steindl's conceptual framework, like Kalecki's, is couched in terms made familiar by the Keynesians on the one hand and the noncompetitive market theorists on the other. The truth is that the orthodox economists, including the Keynesians, were not equipped to understand what Steindl was trying to do and had no standards by which to judge it.[9]

It might be objected that the vogue of economic development in the postwar period contradicts the foregoing analysis. With academic curricula stuffed with courses on development, and textbooks and treatises on the subject adorning every publisher's catalogue, how can it be said that the established profession is not interested in historic trends, "laws of motion," and so on? The answer is simple. The way bourgeois economics treats development is a confirmation of the analysis, not a refutation. The subject is always (so far as I am aware) interpreted to mean the development of underdeveloped (i.e., precapitalist or partially formed capitalist) societies. The questions asked revolve around possible and/or desirable methods of getting them on the road to development, i.e., on the road to becoming advanced capitalist societies. The further they progress along this road, the more they will resemble the Western European and North American societies and the more their economies will behave accordingly. Somewhere along the way, they will be able to throw away the textbooks of economic development and settle down to a steady fare of the latest edition of Samuelson's *Economics*. All of this is merely a modernized version of classical political economy's concern with how society progresses from a rude state of nature peopled by deer and beaver hunters to its final perfected form in the bourgeois paradise of nineteenth-century England. In neither case is any serious attention paid to real historical processes, and in both cases the final outcome is the negation of development.

Keynes not only did nothing to overcome this profoundly antihistorical character of received economic theory; on the contrary, his example and prestige did much to strengthen it.[10] It is therefore really no cause for surprise that Keynes' followers were incapable of transcending his strictly limited vision of capitalist reality. Nor, considering the usual relation between master and epigone, can we say that it is a cause of surprise that in vital respects they took a long step back from the position occupied by Keynes. He was deeply convinced that capitalism is *not* a system of economic harmonics and that its gravest failing was precisely its chronic tendency to depression and stagnation. His followers, with one or two honorable exceptions, cheerfully abandoned this disturbing and at the same time challenging view and gave themselves over to comforting speculations about full-employment equilibria, warranted growth rates, and similar fancies.

Now that stagnation is once again with us, at least in the most advanced and monopolistic of the capitalist countries, now that its abeyance during the forties and early fifties can be clearly seen to have been the result of war, the aftermath of war, and preparation for war—now that these things are being driven home by practical experience to even the dullest observer of the current economic scene, the stage would seem to be set for bourgeois economics to attempt a new step forward. And indeed the need is clearly beginning to be recognized, as evidenced, for example, by the publication of a special issue entitled "Time for a Keynes" by the *New Republic*,[11] organ of the Establishment liberals of the Kennedy era. Whether the need is also beginning to be met is unfortunately more doubtful. The *New Republic*'s contributors include some of the most distinguished names in the U.S. economics profession, and yet, as Professor Hansen says in his "Comment of a Keynesian," they "do not suggest even remotely the emergence of a new economics."[12] It may not be out of place to suggest that before this could happen, bourgeois economics would first have to recover the ground lost since Keynes—to recapture his vision of capitalism, not as the best of all possible worlds but as a system of profound contradictions and deeply rooted self-destructive tendencies.

It may also not be out of place to ask whether this is at all possible in the epoch of the competition of the systems, when the new socialist society is actually challenging capitalism's world leadership. Bourgeois economics, I fear, has irrevocably committed itself to what Marx called "the bad conscience and evil intent of apologetic."[13] If I am right, Keynes may turn out to be its last great representative, and further scientific progress will have to come from the socialist camp (though not necessarily from the socialist countries).

In conclusion, I would like to single out a very minor aspect of the *General Theory* as deserving of special emphasis and commendation a quarter of a century later. "Too large a proportion of recent 'mathematical economics,'" Keynes wrote, "are mere concoctions, as imprecise as the initial assumptions they rest on, which allow the author to lose sight of the complexities and interdependencies of the real world in a maze of pretentious and unhelpful symbols."[14] If this was true in 1936, how much more so is it today when the capacity to generate symbols is becoming the officially recognized criterion of a "good" economist. If it be said that a mathematical ignoramus like myself has no right to entertain or express such views, my answer is simple. Let the enthusiasts tell us what new and important steps forward in the understanding of capitalism have resulted from the mass production of symbols in recent years. Until they do, I shall continue to think that Keynes was fully justified in dismissing what he somewhat contemptuously referred to as the "pseudo-mathematical method."[15] Only it is now necessary to add that what could perhaps have been considered a harmless fad twenty-five years ago has today taken on the dimensions of a disease threatening the health of the entire economics profession.

It is perhaps necessary to add that I intend no blanket criticism of the use of mathematics in economics, nor, I feel sure, did Keynes. Properly used, mathematics can be very valuable, especially as a check on results arrived at by nonmathematical reasoning. Still less am I attempting to disparage the important work that has been done and is being done toward developing mathematical planning and programming techniques. These techniques promise to be enormously valuable to planned socialist societies and undoubtedly have some, if much more limited, applicability to capitalist enterprises and governments. I would only add in this connection that how-to-do-it work of this sort, however useful and even indispensable, should not be confused with the scientific endeavor to *understand* the *modus operandi* of human societies.

Whatever else may be said of Keynes, he was thoroughly committed to that endeavor. Younger economists (and other social scientists) today would do well to heed his example and his advice.

Notes:

1. The reference is to an article, "John Maynard Keynes," which appeared in *Science & Society,* Fall 1946. That article was reprinted in Paul M. Sweezy, *The Present as History,* 2d. ed. (New York: Monthly Review Press, 1970) and later in Lekachman, ed., *Keynes' General Theory.*
2. Such a canvassing of Keynes' writings for light on the long-run determinants of the inducement to invest is reported on by Alan Sweezy, "Declining Investment Opportunity," in *The New Economics,* ed. S. E. Harris (New York: Augustus Kelley, 1947).
3. Arthur Smithies, "The American Economy in the Thirties," *American Economic Review,* May 1946.
4. I am precluded from suggesting ideological prejudice as a major factor since I do not recall that the need for a reconstruction of macro theory in monopolistic terms occurred to any of us at the time, whether we were on the left or on the right or in the center.
5. Joan Robinson, *Economic Philosophy* (Chicago: Aldine Publishing Co., 1962), p. 93.
6. Cf. his *Theory of Economic Dynamics,* p. 161. This is essentially a new and revised edition of two books written more than a decade earlier.
7. Kalecki believed that the primary cause of the slowing up of the long-run rate of growth was "a decline in the intensity of innovations" (ibid.). This is evidently related to the Keynes-Hansen theory discussed above and is subject to the same criticisms.
8. Paul A. Baran, *The Political Economy of Growth* (New York: Monthly Review Press, 1957).
9. The enthusiastic welcome accorded to Steindl's work by a Marxist like Baran can be explained by a similar line of reasoning. What really defines a school of economic thought is the problems it focuses on rather than the particular conceptual apparatus it employs. Thus Marx used the classical concepts of value, profit, rent, etc., with relatively unimportant modifications, though no one would think of calling him a classical economist. These facts have been obscured in recent times, at least among Marxists, by a tendency, particularly strong in the Stalin period, to judge orthodoxy by what may be called the external aspects of a theorist's work rather than by its substance.
10. This is excellently symbolized by the way his remark, so

contemptuous of history, that "in the long run we are all dead" is
quoted *ad nauseam* as a piece of profound wisdom.

11. "Time for a Keynes," *The New Republic,* October 20, 1962.
12. Ibid., pp. 28-29.
13. Marx, *Capital,* Vol. I, "Preface to Second Edition."
14. *General Theory,* p. 298.
15. Ibid., pp. 275, 297.

Power Elite or
Ruling Class?

There is a sort of contrived bloodlessness about American academic social science today. Its practitioners are much better trained than they used to be, but the consequence is not only technical competence. No less striking is the way they all fit into a few neat molds, like the models of an automobile coming off the factory assembly lines. They talk alike, deal in the same brand of trivialities, and take each other enormously seriously. Above all, there is a kind of tacit conspiracy to banish all really interesting and important issues from the universe of "scientific" discourse.

Against this background, C. Wright Mills, associate professor of sociology at Columbia University, stands out as a man of courage and imagination, an iconoclast who cares little for the sacred cows of university administrators and foundation trustees, an innovator who wants to get along with the important business of understanding the United States of America in the middle of the twentieth century. In *White Collar: The American Middle Classes*,[1] he explored the

This article appeared in the September 1956 issue of *Monthly Review*.

emotional and cultural wastelands of American society. Now, in *The Power Elite,*[2] he goes a step further and asks who really runs the show and what makes them tick. The result is an absorbing book that has the added fascination which always attaches to forbidden topics.

The plan of Mills' book is as follows: He opens with a chapter ("The Higher Circles") which gives a general sketch of the theme of the work as a whole. There then follow nine chapters devoted to analyzing the Higher Circles from various angles and by various breakdowns: "Local Society," "Metropolitan 400," "The Celebrities," "The Very Rich," "The Chief Executives," "The Corporate Rich," "The Warlords," "The Military Ascendancy," and "The Political Directorate." Finally come five chapters of interpretation and argumentation: "The Theory of Balance," "The Power Elite," "The Mass Society," "The Conservative Mood," and "The Higher Immorality." There is no compelling logic to the organization of the material, and rigor and elegance are not among Mills' outstanding virtues as a writer. The result is that the book contains not a few asides and excursions, much repetition, and considerable excess verbiage. The whole work would have benefited from a severe editing, and its impact on the reader would, I think, have been sharpened and intensified if it had been cut by, say, a quarter to a third.

Perhaps the greatest merit of *The Power Elite* is that it boldly breaks the taboo which respectable intellectual society has imposed on any serious discussion of how and by whom America is ruled. Those of us who inhabit what may be called the radical underworld have of course never been constrained by this particular taboo, but it must be admitted that radicals have produced very little of scientific value in recent years, and even work that does meet minimum standards of competence has been pretty effectively smothered. In contrast, *The Power Elite,* written by a professor at a respectable university and brought out by a properly conservative publishing house, has already been widely reviewed in such media as *Time* and the *Saturday Review of Literature,* and seems certain to provoke controversy among Mills' professional colleagues. For the first time in a long while, the literate public has been exposed to a serious discussion of social power and stratification at the national—as distinct from the local—level, and currently fashionable theories of the dispersal of power among many groups and interests have been bluntly challenged as flimsy apologetics. This is all to the good, and we may hope that Mills' example will be not only heeded but also emulated by other academic authors and established publishers.[3]

The fact that it raises crucially important issues is by no means the only merit of *The Power Elite.* Indeed, a reviewer cannot pretend even to list all the book's many excellencies: to appreciate them, one must read and study it with the care it deserves. But I do want to call attention to certain features which struck at least one reader as particularly noteworthy:

(1) There are numerous flashes of insight and happy formulations which not only enliven the narrative but, more important, help us to understand difficult or obscure problems. It would be hard to find a more just or damning description of our postwar intellectuals than "those who have abandoned criticism for the new American celebration" (p. 25). It is more than merely salutary to be reminded that "class consciousness is not equally characteristic of all levels of American society: it is most apparent in the upper class" (p. 30). Much of the restless movement of the United States today is illuminated by the statement: "To succeed is to leave local society behind—although certification by it may be needed in order to be selected for national cliques" (p. 39). How vividly the connection between wealth and social standing comes out in this remark: "All families would seem to be rather 'old,' but not all of them have possessed wealth for at least two but preferably three or four generations" (p.

49). And how very apt and accurate is the designation of our present-day corporate system as an "apparatus of appropriation" (p. 107) which showers on its beneficiaries all kinds of blessings in addition to their take-home pay. (Mills is right to emphasize this theme in several different contexts: my only criticism is that he doesn't emphasize it enough.) These are but a few random samples, taken from the first quarter of *The Power Elite,* of what I mean by "flashes of insight and happy formulations." They are among the real pleasures and rewards of the book.

(2) Equally impressive is the factual material which Mills has assembled and analyzed in support or illustration of his arguments. He has made good use of the specialized work of social scientists—for example, A. B. Hollingshead's *Elmtown's Youth*[4] and Dixon Wecter's *The Saga of American Society*[5] — but for the most part he relies on original research in the current press and biographical sources. In this connection, he presents a number of statistical and semi-statistical studies which are important contributions in their own right and which should go far toward exploding some of the more popular and persistent myths about the rich and the powerful in America today. Chapter 5, "The Very Rich," is essentially such a study, and there are others of somewhat less ambitious nature in most of the chapters which undertake to categorize and describe the "power elite." Mills is well aware that an individual researcher, even with considerable help from friends, students, and assistants, can hardly hope to do more than scratch the surface of the vast amount of relevant material which exists in this country; he was, in fact, frequently obliged to put drastic limits on the scope of his efforts. Nevertheless, his factual statements are for the most part solidly, if not exhaustively, supported; and in a field which is not likely to benefit from the generosity (or curiosity) of the well-heeled foundations, we shall probably have to remain content with the contributions of individual

researchers. One could only wish that they were all as careful, competent, and imaginative as Mills.

(3) It seems to me that Mills speaks with the voice of an authentic American radicalism. He is highly critical of the American system and frequently lays about him with strong adjectives, heavy sarcasm, and biting invective. But he doesn't *hate* the "American way of life" and turn his back on it, as so many of our foreign critics do; and he isn't overawed by foreign authority, as so many of our native radicals have always been. One gets the impression that Mills not only understands but to a considerable extent even shares the predominant values of the American "mass society." He indulges in none of the currently fashionable deprecation of "materialism," and his attitude toward wealth is well indicated in a passage which is worth quoting at some length:

> The idea that the millionaire finds nothing but a sad, empty place at the top of society; the idea that the rich do not know what to do with their money; the idea that the successful become filled up with futility, and that those born successful are poor and little as well as rich—the idea, in short, of the disconsolateness of the rich—is, in the main, merely a way by which those who are not rich reconcile themselves to the fact. Wealth in America is directly gratifying and directly leads to many further gratifications.
>
> To be truly rich is to possess the means of realizing in big ways one's little whims and fantasies and sicknesses. "Wealth has great privileges," Balzac once remarked, "and the most enviable of them all is the power of carrying out thoughts and feelings to the uttermost; of quickening sensibility by fulfilling its myriad caprices." The rich, like other men, are perhaps more simply human than otherwise. But their toys are bigger; they have more of them; they have more of them all at once. [Pp. 163-64]

The same idea is more simply summed up in a statement quoted from Sophie Tucker (without either approval or disapproval in the context): "I've been rich and I've been poor, and believe me, rich is best" (p. 346). For a radical, the corollary of this attitude is that it is not wealth that is wrong with America but poverty, and that what is reprehensible about the rich is not that they enjoy the good things of life but that they use their power to maintain a system which needlessly denies the same advantages to others. Mills, to be sure, doesn't spell this out, but I think it is undeniably implicit in his whole position.

It is easy to criticize this point of view, and indeed much of what Mills himself says about the irresponsibility, mind-lessness, and immorality of the "power elite" would furnish the basis of a damning indictment of wealth in a context of exploitation, an indictment which Mills conspicuously fails to elaborate in any thorough or systematic way. But I think that Mills' weaknesses in this connection are characteristically American and that for this reason they have much to teach us about the possibility and requirements of an effective American radical propaganda. Denunciations of wealth as such, in the earlier tradition of radical thought, are likely to fall on deaf ears in this country today: rightly or wrongly, most Americans approve of it and want more for themselves. A successful radical movement must convince them that it really has more of it to offer the great majority of them than has the present system of waste and plunder.

(4) Mills performs a very valuable service in insisting, emphatically and at times even dogmatically, that what happens in the United States today depends crucially on the will and decision of a relatively very small group which is essentially self-perpetuating and responsible to no one but its own membership. And in upholding this position, he earns our gratitude by a forthright attack on the social harmonics of our latter-day Bastiats such as J. K. Galbraith and David

Riesman. Galbraith and Riesman are able social scientists and keen observers of the American scene, but their overall "theories," for which they have received so much praise and fame, are childishly pretentious and superficial. It is high time that a reputable member of the academic community should say so. Some day American social scientists will acknowledge the debt they owe to Mills for having been the first among them to proclaim in no uncertain terms that the king is naked.

I do not mean to imply by this any blanket endorsement of Mills' theoretical contributions. As I hope to show immediately, Mills' theory is open to serious criticism. But he has the very great merit of bringing the real issues into the open and discussing them in a way thay anyone can understand; and he refuses to condone the kind of slick cover-up job that so many of his academic colleagues have been helping to put over on the American and foreign publics in the years of the "American celebration."

It is not easy to criticize *The Power Elite* from a theoretical standpoint for the simple reason that the author often states or implies more than one theory on a given topic or range of topics. Sometimes, I think, this arises from haste in composition and a certain intellectual sloppiness or impatience which seems to characterize much of Mills' work. Sometimes it seems to result from acceptance of the substance as well as the terminology of a kind of "elitist" doctrine which is basically antithetical to the general trend of his thought. And sometimes, no doubt, it arises from the fact that Mills, like most of the rest of us, has not made up his mind about all the problems of American social structure and finds himself with conflicting ideas rattling around in his head. In the brief space available here, I cannot attempt to untangle these confusions and contradictions, nor can I presume to say which of various possible interpretations most accurately reflects Mills' true meaning. Rather, I shall concentrate on trying to show what's wrong with certain ideas, adding in advance an invitation to Mills to correct me to the extent that I am wrong in attributing them to him or to make any other rejoinder he may think called for.

Mills starts off with a concept of the power elite which is disarmingly simple. Those who occupy the "command posts" of our major economic, military, and political institutions constitute the power elite—the big shareholders and executives of the corporate system, the generals and admirals of the Pentagon, and the elected and appointed officials who occupy political positions of national significance. But this of course tells us nothing about the men who stand at these posts—how they got there, their attitudes and values, their relations with each other and with the rest of society, and so on—nor does it provide any but an admittedly misleading clue to these questions: Mills himself repeatedly rejects the notion that the power elite in his sense constitutes some sort of natural aristocracy of ability and intelligence, in spite of the common connotation of the term "elite."

Having in effect defined the power elite as composed of the big shots of industry and government, Mills' next task is to devise a theoretical scheme within which to locate them and to guide his empirical investigations into their characteristics and habits. Two general approaches readily suggest themselves, and Mills follows them both without ever clearly distinguishing them, without asking how far and in what respects they may be in conflict, and without any systematic attempt to reconcile their divergent results. The first approach is via social class: the hypothesis can be put forward and tested that those who occupy the command posts do so as representatives or agents of a national ruling class which trains them, shapes their thought patterns, and selects them for their positions of high responsibility. The second approach is via what Mills variously calls the "major institutional orders" (e.g., on p. 269), the "major hierarchies" (p.

287), the "big three domains" (p. 288), and other more or less synonymous terms. This assumes that there are distinct spheres of social life—the economic, the military, and the political—each with its own institutional structure, that each of these spheres throws up its own leading cadres, and that the top men of all three come together to form the power elite.

Now there may be societies, past or present, in which this idea of more or less autonomous orders, hierarchies, or domains has enough relevance to make it a fruitful approach to problems of social structure and power. But it seems perfectly clear to me that the United States is not and never has been such a society. Moreover, the cumulative effect of the empirical data presented by Mills is decisively against any such interpretation of the American system. He adduces a wealth of material on our class system, showing how the local units of the upper class are made up of propertied families and how these local units are welded together into a wholly self-conscious national class. He shows how the "power elite" is overwhelmingly (and increasingly) recruited from the upper levels of the class system, how the same families contribute indifferently to the economic, military, and political "elites," and how the same individuals move easily and almost imperceptibly back and forth from one to another of these elites. When it comes to "The Political Directorate" (Chapter 10), he demonstrates that the notion of a specifically political elite is in reality a myth, that the crucial positions in government and politics are increasingly held by what he calls "political outsiders," and that these outsiders are in fact members or errand boys of the corporate rich.

This demonstration in effect reduces the "big three" to the "big two"—the corporate and the military domains. There is no doubt at all about the decisive importance of the former, and Mills makes some of his most useful and interesting contributions in discussing the wealth, power, and other characteristics of the corporate rich.[6] But the evidence for an autonomous, or even semi-autonomous, military domain of comparable importance is so weak that it can be said to be almost nonexistent. Historically, to be sure, the military has normally been somewhat separated from the mainstream of American life, and in this sense one could perhaps speak of a military domain. But it has been small and completely subject to civilian control, quite impotent in terms of the national decision-making which is the special function of Mills' power elite. In wartime, of course, the military has swelled enormously in size and power, but it is precisely then that it has ceased to be a separate domain. The civilian higher circles have moved into commanding military positions, and the top brass has been accepted into the higher circles. What happens in such times is that the power elite becomes militarized in the sense that it has to concern itself with military problems, it requires military skills, and it must inculcate in the underlying population greater respect for military virtues and personnel.

All this has nothing in common with the rise to power of a military order headed by an elite of "warlords," though it is in these terms that Mills describes what has been happening in the United States since the beginning of the Second World War, and indeed *must* describe it or else abandon the whole theory of a composite power elite made up of separate "domainal" elites; for on his own showing the "political directorate" is merely an emanation of the corporate rich. To support the theory of "The Warlords" (Chapter 8) and "The Military Ascendancy" (Chapter 9), Mills brings forth little evidence beyond the well-known facts that the military trade has traditionally required a specialized training and code of conduct, and that the Pentagon is an important center of power in American life. But these facts require no such fancy interpretation and are perfectly compatible with a more prosaic theory of the locus of power in mid-twentieth-century United States.

But Mills really relies much less on facts than on a sort of unstated syllogism to back up his warlord-military ascendancy theory. The syllogism might be formulated as follows: the major outlines of American policy, both foreign and domestic, are drawn in terms of a "military definition of world reality" which has been accepted by the power elite as a whole; this military definition of reality (also referred to as "military metaphysics") must be the product of the professional military mind ("the warlords"); *ergo* the warlords now occupy a decisive position within the power elite ("the military ascendancy"). This may look impressive and convincing at a first glance, but a moment's reflection will show that it explains nothing and constitutes no support whatever for Mills' theory. Professional military people naturally think in military terms and have doubtless always tried to persuade others to see things their way. Throughout most of U.S. history, they have succeeded, if at all, only in wartime. The real problem is to understand why it is that since the Second World War the whole power elite has come to think increasingly in military terms and hence to accord a place of greater honor and power to the military. Without an answer to this, all the facts that seem to Mills to add up to the military ascendancy of the warlords remain quite unexplained.

Now Mills himself never faces up to this question, and the only relevant answer I can find is that the United States now, unlike in the past, lives in a "military neighborhood" (the phrase is used on a number of occasions), which presumably means that the country is under constant threat (or potential threat) of attack and military defeat. This is more sophisticated than saying that we live in mortal danger of red aggression, but its explanatory value is exactly the same: in either case the increasing militarization of American life is the result of external forces. The rise of the warlords, then, is seen as the outcome of a world historical process for which the United States has no responsibility and over which it has no control, and not, as Mills clearly wants to prove, as the outcome of *internal* forces operating in the military domain.

Thus, while Mills appears to have little in common with the cold war liberals, and in fact rather generally holds them in contempt, his theory of the role of the military leads to very much the same conclusions. I believe that this is no accident. "Elitist" thinking *inevitably* diverts attention from problems of social structure and process and leads to a search for external causes of social phenomena. Simon-pure elitists like Pareto and his followers frankly adopt this method and find what they are looking for in the alleged natural qualities of their elites. Semi-elites like Mills—people who think they can adopt the terminology without any of the basic ideas of elitist theory—tend to get bogged down in confusion from which the only escape is to borrow the most banal ideas of their opponents.

It is too bad that Mills gets into this kind of a mess, because as I indicated above, his work is strongly influenced by a straightforward class theory which, if he had stuck to it and consistently explored its implications, would have enabled him to avoid completely the superficialities and pitfalls of elitist thinking. The uppermost class in the United States is, and long has been, made up of the corporate rich who directly pull the economic levers. Prior to the Great Depression and the Second World War, the corporate rich left political and military matters largely (though by no means exclusively) in the control of hired hands and trusted agents; but since the highly dangerous economic breakdown of the thirties, the Big Boys have increasingly taken over the key positions themselves. Their unwillingness to solve the economic programs of capitalism through a really massive welfare state program meant that they welcomed the war as the salvation of their system. Since the end of the Second World

War, they have accepted, nay created and sold through all the media of mass communications, a "military definition of reality" as the ideological-political underpinning of the war-preparations economy, which remains crucial to the whole profit-making mechanism on which their wealth and power rests. For this purpose, they have lavishly subsidized and encouraged the military, which in turn has not only grown vastly in size but also has been enormously flattered and has become the most loyal defender and promoter of the "free enterprise" system. The picture of warlords exercising a military ascendancy is fanciful: *our* warlords have no fundamental values or purposes different from those of their corporate colleagues; many of them perform virtually indistinguishable jobs; and the crowning achievement of a military career today is the board chairmanship of a billion-dollar corporation.[7] At the same time, we have nothing even approaching a unified military order or caste seeking to impose its "military metaphysics" on the nation. The most famous of our "warlords," President Eisenhower, is now the most peaceful of our influential politicians; while our most strident "militarists" are civilian Senators Symington and Jackson whose closest affiliations would seem to be with the multi-billion-dollar aircraft industry.

No, the facts simply won't fit Mills' theory of three (or two) sectional elites coming together to form an overall power elite. What we have in the United States is a *ruling class* with its roots deeply sunk in the "apparatus of appropriation" which is the corporate system. To understand this ruling class—its metaphysics, its purposes, and its morals—we need to study, not certain "domains" of American life, however defined, but the whole system of monopoly capitalism.

A large part of Mills' theory and most of his facts support this view. This, indeed, is why his book, for all its weaknesses, is such a vital and powerful document. Let us hope that in the future he will drop *all* the elitist nonsense and make the contribution he is capable of making to deepening our theory and understanding of the American class system.[8]

In conclusion, I should like to comment very briefly on four of the many issues which would merit detailed discussion in a full-dress review of *The Power Elite:*

(1) Because he blurs the whole problem of class and class relations, Mills fails to throw any but incidental light on the dynamics of the class system—how people lose high-class status, how new members of the ruling class are co-opted, and so on. In this connection, he completely fails to understand the role of the preparatory schools and colleges as recruiters for the ruling class, sucking upward the ablest elements of the lower classes and thus performing the double function of infusing new brains into the ruling class and weakening the potential leadership of the working class. It is this aspect of the American educational system, involving as it does fairly generous scholarships and other forms of assistance for the bright poor, which is most often and least deservedly praised as democratic.

(2) While Mills' chapter on "The Celebrities" is informative and amusing, it is a hopeless muddle from the theoretical point of view. The celebrities—of screen, TV, radio, stage, sport—are not an integral part of the ruling class or the power elite, and in general they do not compete in prestige with the rich and the powerful. On the contrary, the rich and the powerful have every interest in building up the celebrities, partly because it is good business and partly to divert the attention of the underlying population from more serious matters. This is all part of what Mills elsewhere calls, in a memorable phrase, "the grim trivialization of American life." Mills' confusion on these questions—which of course does not prevent him from saying many true and penetrating things about them—stems in large part from the lack of any clear or

usable theory of prestige. He treats prestige as a pure magnitude and quite misses the point that there are different kinds as well as quantities of prestige and that they have different bases and perform different functions in the social structure.

(3) I pointed out above that Mills strongly insists, quite rightly in my view, that major national decisions in this country are made by a relatively small group of people at the top of the social pyramid. But in his concern to drive this point home, it seems to me that he goes much too far in the direction of what I may call "historical voluntarism." In *The Power Elite,* Mills makes the following statement:

> It is . . . true that if most men and women take whatever roles are permitted to them and enact them as they are expected to by virtue of their position, this is precisely what the elite need *not* do, and often do not do. They may call into question the structure, their position within it, or the way they are to enact that position. [P. 24]

If this were *really* true, our only hope of understanding the behavior of the top group would be through psychoanalysis: the objectively discoverable pressures and compulsions of the social order which operate on the rest of us would be irrelevant to these august Olympians. But of course it is not true, and I make so bold as to say that most of the time Mills himself knows it perfectly well. What corporation executive can afford to order his behavior without regard to his company's profit-and-loss statement? What American politician today can flout the interests of the corporate rich who put him in office? What military man can say that the Soviet Union is no menace and the United States should set the world an example of unilateral disarmament? To be sure, each one of these gentlemen can behave in the indicated fashion, provided he is prepared to lose his job and with it his power. But this is precisely the point: like everyone else, the elite have roles to perform, and for the most part they are exacting ones: failure means loss of position and power.

What Mills could and should have argued in this connection is that the roles are *not* like those of a theatrical performance, completely mapped out and rigidly determined in advance. The actors have a *range of choice* which is set by the nature and laws of the social structure under which they live, and this range may even include such fateful alternatives as that which faced Harry Truman in August 1945, whether or not to drop a bomb that would in a single flash snuff out the lives of a quarter of a million human beings. "Men make their own history," Marx wrote in the *Eighteenth Brumaire,* "but they do not make it just as they please; they do not make it under circumstances chosen by themselves, but under circumstances directly found, given and transmitted from the past." That is the simple truth, confirmed by mountains of historical and personal experience alike. Why can't social scientists as reasonable and sensible as C. Wright Mills take it in *and hold onto it?*

(4) Finally, a word about a matter which has undoubtedly disturbed some left-wing readers of *The Power Elite.* Mills, they say, explodes many myths about the United States today. He shows that the country is run by a tiny irresponsible minority, and that in crucial respects the consequence is a drift from bad to worse. But he says nothing at all about what can or should be done about it.

For my part, I see no valid ground for criticism here. We should be grateful for such a good book, and we can draw our own conclusions about what to do about the situation it reveals. We can even go farther and commend Mills for his restraint: we know from his association with the magazine *Dissent* that Mills considers himself a socialist, and we can be pretty sure that under present circumstances *The Power Elite* with explicitly stated socialist conclusions would never have been published, reviewed, and read as it has been without the conclusions.

For the rest, it is no violation of principle not to set down everything in your mind every time you put pen to paper. What *is* a violation of principle is to set down a lot of things that aren't true or you don't believe, and on this score, so far as I am able to judge, Mills deserves a clean bill of health.

Notes:

1. C. Wright Mills, *White Collar: The American Middle Classes* (New York: Oxford University Press, 1956).
2. Mills, *The Power Elite* (New York: Oxford University Press, 1956).
3. Let me take this occasion to express a subsidiary hope that writers like Mills will become even bolder in challenging the taboos of respectability. Ever since it was founded in 1949, *Monthly Review* has consistently sought to analyze and clarify the problems of *national* power in American society—not, I hope, without throwing out some useful and interesting suggestions. Mills makes generous reference in his notes to our analysis of "The Roots and Prospects of McCarthyism" (*Monthly Review,* January 1954) but otherwise fails to note, even in a bibliographical way, any of the numerous articles and editorials which have dealt with one or more aspects of his chosen subject. Of course, it is possible that Mills may not be familiar with this material or may consider it of no value. A more likely explanation of his ignoring it, I think, is a (perhaps unconscious) fear of what might be called "guilt by citation." At any rate, this fear is certainly common enough in academic circles nowadays, whether or not it was operative in Mills' case. From the point of view of the "power elite," it serves the useful purpose of helping to isolate radicals and censor radical thought. From the point of view of scientific discussion and advance, needless to say, its effects are wholly negative.
4. A. B. Hollingshead, *Elmtown's Youth* (New York: John Wiley, 1949).
5. Dixon Wecter, *The Saga of American Society* (New York: Charles Scribner, 1970).

6. The three chapters entitled "The Very Rich," "The Chief Executives," and "The Corporate Rich" are not really about different groups. They are simply about differently constructed but widely overlapping samplings of what is essentially a homogeneous social stratum which can be aptly designated as "the corporate rich."

7. On this whole range of topics, see the fascinating article entitled "They're Masters of Buying by the Billion," *Business Week,* June 23, 1956. "They" are Generals C. S. Irvine and E. W. Rawlings, in charge of procurement and supply for the air force. Mr. Dudley C. Sharp, civilian assistant secretary of the air force, is quoted as saying: "These two could run any business in the world. They're absolutely the finest executives I've ever met." Chances are, too, that they will end up running one or more of the world's biggest businesses!

8. Mills' reasons for rejecting the ruling class concept are stated in a footnote (p. 277) which deserves no more than a footnote in reply. "Ruling class," he says, is a "badly loaded" phrase in the sense that it contains the theory that "an economic class rules politically." What of it? The question is whether the theory is applicable to the United States today, and if investigation shows that it is, then the only "loading" is on the side of truth. As I have argued above, most of Mills' factual material supports the ruling class theory to the hilt—provided only that one doesn't insist on interpreting the words "economic" and "class" in an impossibly narrow and tortured way. For the rest, I have already said enough about Mills' alternative theory, repeated in the footnote in question, that a "coalition" of the "higher agents" of the "three domains" constitutes a power elite. (There is, of course, no loading at all in the phrase "power elite"!)

Thoughts on the
American System

A change of administration usually provides useful insights into the nature and mode of functioning of the U.S. social order, and in this respect the accession to power of the Nixon regime is no exception.

First of all, we can see from Nixon's cabinet appointments how monopoly capitalism tends to rely increasingly for its top functionaries and administrators on men whose chief training and experience have been either in managing and manipulating capital in its most abstract forms or in servicing the system as a whole. In the former category we include bankers and corporation lawyers, in the latter university professors. The Nixon cabinet—counting as members the director of the budget bureau and the presidential assistants in the fields of national security and urban affairs—contains two Wall Street lawyers, three bankers, and four professors, altogether nine out of the total of fifteen. Of the remaining six, four rose to the top as businessmen and only two as politicians. What appear likely to be the four key

This article appeared in the February 1969 issue of *Monthly Review*.

policy-making positions—Attorney General and the Secretaries of State, Defense, and Treasury—are occupied by two lawyers, one politician, and one banker. On the whole, the "generalists," in the sense of those whose main concern has been the system as a whole rather than specific interests within the system, appear to be firmly in the saddle. And this both reflects and is in accord with the nature of an economy that is increasingly dominated by a few hundred giant multinational corporations which need a government to serve their common interests both at home and abroad much more than they need a government which favors some sectors of the economy or regions of the country at the expense of others.

Secondly, the composition of the Nixon cabinet clearly shows up the artificiality of the theory, expounded by C. Wright Mills,[1] that there are separate business and political "domains" each with its own "elite." The very fact that 60 percent of the cabinet members have essentially business backgrounds is in conflict with the theory of a separate political domain. Furthermore, most of this substantial majority have had extensive previous governmental experience. The new Secretary of the Treasury, chairman of the biggest bank in Chicago, started off as an official of the Federal Reserve System; the new Secretary of State, a Wall Street lawyer, served as Attorney General under Eisenhower; three of four businessmen appointed to lesser cabinet posts have been state governors; and so on.

It is of course true that there are corporate and government bureaucracies between which there may be, *on the whole,* relatively little mobility; and in this sense one can speak of separate business and political domains. Many, perhaps even most, top positions in politics are filled by people who made it in business. And people who make it in politics usually find many lucrative jobs in business open to them (Nixon himself is a good example of this: in 1962 he

temporarily abandoned a political career for the senior
partnership in one of the big Wall Street law firms). What we
find at the top, in other words, is a small ruling *class* whose
members either themselves occupy the positions of power or
select and hence control those who do. And these members
and their positions are essentially interchangeable.

While we are on the subject of elites, there is another
aspect of C. Wright Mills' theory which is in need of
re-examination in the light of the experience of the last few
years. In his schema there are not just two domains with their
elites but three—corporate, political, and military. At the
time Mills' book appeared, we had no hesitation in rejecting
the idea for the military as well as for the corporate and
political.[2] In the long sweep of American history, the
constitutional principle of civilian control over the military
had never been successfully challenged. What this principle
means of course is that the military, like the police, is an
instrument of the ruling class and not an independent center
of power: its job is to do what it is told to, leaving
policy-making to the representatives of the bourgeoisie. The
showdown between President Truman and General Mac-
Arthur over the limits and aims of the Korean War showed
that the principle of civilian control had survived the Second
World War, the beginnings of the cold war, and the Korean
War. But this same incident also revealed a powerful
tendency within the military to assert itself as a policy-
making center. And there is no question that the massive
military buildup of the Kennedy-Johnson era plus the
increasing U.S. involvement in the Vietnam war have greatly
strengthened the hand of the military. The question is
whether this process has gone so far that the military is now
in a position to enforce its will on the civilian leadership with
respect to matters which the military regards as its own
particular concern. If the answer is yes, it would follow that
Mills' theory of a military elite sharing power has validity,

regardless of whether we accept or reject the notion of separate corporate and political elites. For there is no doubt that there is such a thing as a military domain in Mills' sense, or that it does select and train its own leadership: making it in business or politics does not provide a ticket of admission to the Top Brass.[3]

The composition of the Nixon administration does not provide any convincing clues to the answer to this question. It is certainly interesting that for the first time since its creation immediately after the Second World War, the Department of Defense has been put in the charge of a politician. Since Truman's administration, this post has been held by the president or board chairman of the following corporations: General Motors, Proctor and Gamble, Morgan Guaranty Trust, and Ford. In other words, the Department of Defense has normally been in the charge of a top executive of one of the country's biggest corporations, the kind of person who could presumably most effectively enforce civilian control on the military. The fact that Nixon has chosen as his Secretary of Defense a small-town Middle Western politician with notoriously hawkish views,[4] suggests an intention to give the military its head.

But this is not the only possible hypothesis. It might also be reasoned that the U.S. ruling class has decided to put an end to the war in Vietnam and that this decision can be made more palatable to hawks, both in and out of the Pentagon, if one of their own is given major responsibility for implementing it and coping with its consequences.[5] This line of reasoning of course assumes that real power is entirely in civilian hands.

What makes it so difficult to establish the truth here is the fact that there is in any case such a wide area of agreement between the leadership of the giant corporations and the military elite. Both *want* a huge war machine, but the former *needs* it even more than the latter. This need is based on both international and domestic considerations. The defense of the U.S. empire, alias the "free world," is quite literally a life-and-death matter for a large number of the biggest corporations; and for the entire ruling class massive (and growing) government spending on the war machine is the only acceptable form of surplus utilization on the scale required to keep the U.S. economy from sinking back into the kind of stagnation and mass unemployment which characterized the years of the Great Depression. It follows that the mere fact that the military gets practically everything it asks for in no way proves that it is an independent power center. The ruling class built the war machine up from the low point to which it was reduced by the hasty demobilization right after the Second World War, to serve its own global purposes and not to please the generals and admirals. The question whether, in the process, the generals and admirals have acquired real power in their own right is therefore not one which can be answered according to any simple criteria of size and rate of growth of the war machine.

A real test may come over the issue of ending the Vietnam war. If, as seems to be widely assumed, the ruling class is now ready to write Vietnam off, it may well meet bitter resistance from the military, determined to hang on at the cost of endless fighting and possibly even of war with China. In this way a power struggle might be precipitated, the outcome of which would decide whether or not the traditional American principle of civilian control over the military is still in operation.

Whether this will actually happen, however, is another question. What is at issue is not whether the ruling class *wants* to end the Vietnam war (of course it does), but whether it is now ready to do so on the only terms which can bring peace to that country. These terms have long been well known to those who are not blinded by class interests and ideology: complete withdrawal of U.S. armed forces from Vietnam. This of course implies the end of the Saigon puppet regime and the takeover of power in all of South Vietnam by the National Liberation Front (and its allies) which is already in control of most of the countryside. What evidence is there that the U.S. ruling class has reconciled itself to this prospect?

If there is any such evidence, we frankly do not know what it is. The actual course of events has proved that Johnson's withdrawal from the presidential race and subsequent opening of negotiations with Hanoi together constituted an extremely effective method of undermining and disorienting the domestic antiwar movement. It seems only reasonable, therefore, to assume that this, rather than peace, was the intended purpose. And of course Nixon is not going to abandon such a well-tested tactic: it seems that Americans by and large are willing to tolerate and perhaps even support the war if it is accompanied by sufficiently well advertised "peace" talks.[6] Meanwhile, all the pronouncements we have run across emanating from what may be called "responsible" ruling-class quarters continue to take it for granted that South Vietnam, with or without the present Saigon regime, will remain a U.S. client state after the war is over. This is true even of statements, like the well-publicized one by McGeorge Bundy a couple of months ago, which appear to be most emphatic on the overriding need to end the war. The U.S. ruling class, it seems, simply has not absorbed the lesson of the last fifteen years, that it is impossible to establish a viable neocolony in South Vietnam.

This does not mean, to be sure, that the lesson never will be learned or, even if it isn't, that U.S. forces will remain in Vietnam forever. But "never" and "forever" are not very precise terms and certainly do not rule out a long period of maneuvering by the United States to find a way to impose its will on Vietnam. Already we are being bombarded once again with optimistic stories, coming from both Saigon and Washington, about how well the war is going, how many villages and districts have been pacified, how rapidly the morale of the Saigon troops is rising and that of the NLF falling, and so on *ad nauseam*. What seems to be happening in fact is that U.S. and puppet forces are withdrawing more and more into fortified bases and urban enclaves (the latter increasingly infiltrated by enemy cadres), while the NLF-held countryside is subjected to stepped-up B-52 bombing. If this is correct, it means that the United States is actually adopting, without acknowledging it, the so-called enclave strategy which has been advocated in the last few years by such men as Generals Gavin and Ridgway, Messrs. Kennan and Galbraith, and Senators Fulbright and McGovern.

How long this will go on is a question no one can answer. Presumably it *can* go on for a long time yet: even Wilfred Burchett, the leading English-speaking reporter and analyst of Vietnamese victories, does not assert, in his writings in the *Guardian* and in his new book *Vietnam Will Win!*,[7] that the Vietnamese are in a position literally to throw the U.S. forces out of Vietnam. They will leave Vietnam only when a decision is taken in Washington to pull them out. And what combination of pressures—from new "Tet offensives" in South Vietnam, from military explosions in other parts of the world, from renewed international monetary crises, from rising urban rebellions at home, from a revived antiwar movement inside the United States—will convince the U.S. ruling class that the Vietnam game is not worth the candle, this too is a question no one can answer. If and when the time does arrive, the next problem facing the ruling class may be to try to persuade its own military to go along.

If that happens we shall at any rate have a real test of the theory that the military has become an independent power center in U.S. society.

Let us now turn to another aspect of the American system, the internal power structure. In matters of international and military policy there is no doubt that all power is in the hands of the federal government and, within the federal government, increasingly in the hands of the executive branch. (We say "increasingly," but "exclusively" might be more accurate: it is hard to cite an instance in recent years in which the Senate or the Congress as a whole has had a visible influence in shaping foreign or military policies.) In domestic affairs the situation is different and much more complicated.

To begin with, we must bear in mind that the governmental structure of the United States makes a sharp distinction between the federal government on the one hand and the state and local governments on the other. While the distribution of functions among the different levels cannot be precisely defined, and indeed is subject to continuous dispute and recurring judicial determination, nevertheless each level does have a large area of responsibility in which it makes and carries out policy in relative independence of the others. The dangers inherent in this system are obvious: unless the same interests hold power at all three levels, discordant or even contradictory policies may be adopted, resulting in serious impairment of the functioning of the system as a whole.

How is it in the United States today: do the same interests hold power at all three levels? (It is worth noting in passing that in most of the other advanced capitalist countries this problem does not arise since the central government directly controls the regional and local governments.) In a very general sense, yes: large property owners or their representatives hold power at all three levels. They are all therefore interested in maintaining the system and in maximizing U.S. power and wealth vis-à-vis the rest of the world. This explains why, on matters of foreign and military policy, there is normally general agreement among the various sections of the ruling class: the corporate rich in control of the central government pursue their collective interests with the enthusiastic support of their lesser colleagues in the regions and localities.

When it comes to the state and local governments, however, things are not so simple. The headquarters of the economically dominant giant corporations are concentrated in New York and a few other major cities, and the political activities of their top leaders are for the most part concerned with national and international affairs: typically, they play little or no role in state and local politics. Further down the corporate ladder there is a tremendous amount of mobility of both the job and the geographical varieties. The college or university graduate who goes to work for one of the multinational giants can expect to be shifted around from one branch or plant to another, nationally and even internationally, not once but repeatedly in the course of his corporate career. The result is that he never settles in any community long enough to put down roots; he never gains the intimate first-hand acquaintance with local people and problems without which it is impossible to be politically effective. Of course, the giants can and do achieve a measure of political influence at state and local levels through spending money, directly in some cases but more often through their officials, in support of particular politicians or political machines. If they were the only sources of big money for these purposes, they could doubtless achieve outright control of state and local governments. But this is very far from being the case. In every community of any size there are rich, and often very rich, men and women whose primary source of income is ownership of property which is situated and controlled right where they live—family businesses, construction companies, local banks, above all real estate. These people can well afford their own politicians and political machines, and of course it is important to them for a thousand and one reasons to control the governments which are closest to their operations. Given the fact that their local experience and connections are vastly superior to those of the absentee corporate owners and managers, it is not surprising that they pretty well monopolize power at the state and local levels.

We thus have a situation in which the corporate giants control the federal government, and locally based vested interests control the state and local governments. Throughout most of the period when this arrangement has been in operation—i.e., since the rise of Big Business in the last decades of the nineteenth century—it has worked reasonably well for the power-wielders at both levels. The giants, in fact, have for the most part been happy to chase after the profits offered by expanding national and international markets without having to worry about running everything down below. But in recent years inner conflicts and contradictions have been developing which greatly complicate the growing general crisis of U.S. monopoly capitalism.

To understand this one must recall some of the major features of the capital accumulation process in the present phase of U.S. economic development. The greater profitability of the corporate giants provides them with the wherewithal to grow more rapidly than the smaller and more competitive sectors of the economy (this is what Marx called the concentration of capital), and their huge financial resources give them the leverage to engineer an uninterrupted series of mergers (Marx's centralization of capital). Technologically, this increasingly dominant monopolistic sector of the economy is highly dynamic, with a strong bias toward more and more sophisticated, capital-intensive methods of production. The big monopolies, in their search for profitable markets, make available to other sectors of the economy advanced mechanical, electronic, chemical, and other sophisticated devices which in turn revolutionize these sectors' methods of production. In this way, for example, U.S. agriculture has been rapidly mechanized (and chemicalized); and hand labor of the "ditch-digging" type has been virtually eliminated from the construction industry.

These trends and tendencies, together with related developments in such fields as transportation and communication, have had a profound impact on the location of economic activity, the nature of the labor process, and the composition of the work force. Some production centers—particularly in the South, Southwest, and Far West—have burgeoned. The countryside has been drastically depopulated, with displaced farm workers crowding into the cities. Inside the metropolitan areas population has moved steadily out from the city centers to an ever widening periphery, leaving the bottom income groups in decaying slum areas which also tend to expand outward with the increase of population and the growth of the metropolitan area. These slum dwellers in turn are made up of a hereditary lumpenproletariat plus the steadily swelling ranks of rejects from the high-technology economy: migrants from the countryside and technologically unemployed and/or unemployable in the industrial and service sectors. When you add the historically conditioned facts that a large proportion of the central-city low-income stratum is made up of ghettoized blacks (on a nationwide scale) and Puerto Ricans and Mexican-Americans (in certain regions), and that these are the sectors of the U.S. population which are being awakened and stirred into action by the worldwide anti-imperialist revolution of the twentieth century —when you add all this up, you have the ingredients of the two great interlocked crises which are widely recognized as threatening to tear apart the very fabric of U.S. society—the crisis of the cities and the crisis of race relations.

From a narrowly economic point of view these dramatic developments are of little concern to the corporate giants. They have not suffered in any discernible way from the trials and tribulations of the cities: corporate profits after taxes rose from $26.7 billion in 1960 to $48.1 billion in 1967, an average annual increase of more than 10 percent a year. The multinationals have been spreading their tentacles around the globe as never before. Furthermore, the big corporations don't operate in the slums (most of their executives have probably never even been in a slum), nor do they need the kind of unskilled low-paid labor which is available there. The truth is that for corporations which operate on the national and international levels, the problems of the impoverished inner cities are economically irrelevant.

The same cannot be said politically, however. Anything that threatens to disrupt the whole social order, as the urban and race crises unquestionably do, is very much a matter of concern to the corporate giants and the national ruling class which they nurture: they need an environment of civic peace and stability in which to carry on their profitable economic activities. But the question is: what can they do to secure and protect such an environment? And here we meet again what has by now clearly become a major contradiction of the American system.

The big corporations and the national ruling class do not control the state and local governments.[8] Most of what would be necessary to make serious improvements in the cities and to ameliorate racial conflict and rebelliousness within the cities would have to be done at the metropolitan level. Those local property owners who do control the state and local governments, unlike the big corporations, have an enormous stake in the slums and ghettos (as markets, high-yield real estate, sources of cheap labor for marginal businesses and domestic workers, etc.) and have absolutely no intention to sacrifice what are to them vital interests for the sake of creating an environment favorable to the operations of the big corporations and the national ruling class. What is at issue here is very clearly indicated by Hans

Blumenfeld, one of the world's leading authorities in the field of urban planning. Writing in an article entitled "The Modern Metropolis,"[9] Blumenfeld draws the following conclusion:

> Any plan that seeks to control the growth of the metropolis rather than leaving it to the play of market forces will require the setting up of new forms of control. Because it inevitably entails transfers of value from one piece of land to another, planning of any sort is bound to come into conflict with the existing vested interests of landowners and municipalities. It is obvious, therefore, that the implementation of rational regional planning would call for: (1) the creation of an overall metropolitan government for the metropolis, (2) public ownership of all or most of the land that is to be developed, (3) tax revenues sufficient to enable the metropolitan government to acquire the land and carry out the public works required for its development, (4) a national housing policy that would eliminate segregation by providing people at all income levels with freedom of choice in the location of their dwellings.
>
> In terms of current American political folklore these are radical measures. Each of them, however, has been carried out in varying forms and to a varying degree by more than one European nation within the framework of democratic capitalism.

The reason European capitalist nations have been able to carry out such programs is simply that their ruling classes, which are responsible for their national systems as a whole, are in control of regional and local governments. The U.S. ruling class, on the other hand, is saddled with a governmental structure which confers power at the regional and local levels on particularistic interests which have no responsibility for the system as a whole.

In these circumstances urban development will continue to be governed by market forces and to generate conflicts—the current one over New York City's educational system is a good example—which, from the point of view of U.S. monopoly capitalism as a national and international system of making profits and accumulating capital, are totally irrational and destructive.

The national ruling class is obviously extremely reluctant to meet this problem head-on, fearing that any wholesale attack on local vested interests (political as well as economic) would set off even more destructive and dangerous conflicts. So it temporizes, trying to bribe and cajole local power-holders through such devices as federal departments of urban affairs and transportation, Ford Foundations, university institutes of city planning, and the like. The results, as should by now be obvious, have been and will continue to be minimal.

Sooner or later it seems inevitable that more drastic measures will be tried: the problem itself is bound to get steadily worse. But what these measures may be it is now impossible to foresee.

Notes:

1. Mills, *The Power Elite.*
2. See "Power Elite or Ruling Class?" pp. 92-109 above.
3. It is true, however, that retiring generals and admirals are much in demand for leading corporate and political positions. This one-way mobility into the top echelon of the civilian ruling class works against the military's acquiring its own specific values and ambitions.
4. For a thumbnail sketch of Laird's ideas on U.S. global strategy, see *I. F. Stone's Weekly,* December 30, 1968.
5. Writing of French withdrawal from Algeria, Maxime Rodinson comments: "As usually happens, the capitulation to Algerian nationalism, so wounding to the national pride and so harmful to the interests of a large number of Frenchmen, could only be made

acceptable by a right-wing government, or at least one which could not be accused of sacrificing the nation to some universalist ideology. This was the historic role of Charles de Gaulle...." (*Israel and the Arabs* [New York: Pantheon, 1969], p. 137).

6. From the point of view of strengthening the antiwar movement in the United States, the best thing that could happen would be for the Vietnamese to pack up and leave the Paris talks, telling the U.S. delegation to let them know when Washington is ready for serious negotiations. That the Vietnamese do not do this is due to the fact that they have more important aims than strengthening the U.S. antiwar movement, chief of which is to hasten the disintegration of what is left of the Saigon regime.

7. Wilfred Burchett, *Vietnam Will Win!* (New York: A Guardian Book, 1969).

8. The entrance into state politics of men like Governor Nelson Rockefeller of New York and his brother Governor Winthrop Rockefeller of Arkansas may indicate that the national ruling class is trying to take over key positions at the lower levels. The effectiveness of this strategy is doubtful, however. Even a governor or mayor can accomplish little against the vested interests which control state legislatures, city councils, and state and local bureaucracies.

9. *Scientific American,* September 1965.

II
Marx and
Modern Capitalism

Karl Marx and the Industrial Revolution

I have long been greatly impressed by the fact that Karl Marx, though using a conceptual framework derived from and in many ways very similar to classical economic theory, nevertheless reached conclusions radically different from those of the classical economists. Noting that Marx viewed the capitalist process as "one which, in principle, involves ceaseless accumulation accompanied by changes in methods of production," I wrote in 1942:

> It is at once apparent that this view of the capitalist process differs radically from that which underlies the classical theory of economic evolution. The latter is, in principle, unconcerned with changes in methods of production; economic development is viewed exclusively in terms of (gradual) quantitative changes in population, capital, wages, profits, and rent. Social relations remain unaffected; the end product is simply a

Reprinted from Robert V. Eagly, ed., *Events, Ideology and Economic Theory: The Determinants of Progress in the Development of Economic Analysis* (Detroit: Wayne State University Press, 1968), by permission of Wayne State University Press.

state of affairs in which all these rates of change equal zero [the stationary state]. Since the Marxian view lays primary stress on changes in methods of production, it implies qualitative change in social organization and social relations as well as quantitative change in economic variables as such. The way is thus paved for regarding the "end product" as a revolutionary reconstitution of society rather than a mere state of rest.[1]

Part of the explanation of this fundamental difference between Marx and the classics may well lie in the opposing personal and class interests that they represented. But I think it would be a mistake to leave the matter there. Classical political economy, especially in its Ricardian form, was not incompatible with a theory of class conflict: indeed, Ricardo himself pointed out and emphasized the conflict of interest between capitalists and landlords, and the so-called Ricardian socialists soon showed that the theory could equally well be used to underpin a theory of class struggle between capital and labor. Like them, Marx could have espoused the cause of the working class without making any important changes in classical economic theory. That he did not do so but instead transformed classical political economy into a radically new theory of economic development must be explained by something other than, or at any rate additional to, class interest. In what follows I shall try to show that Marx, in contrast to the classics, systematically took into account and incorporated into his theoretical system that interrelated series of events and processes which is generally known as the industrial revolution. Marx's conceptualization of the industrial revolution is, I believe, the basis of his theory of economic development.

Let us begin by noting that Marx used the term "industrial revolution" again and again,[2] not as a mere catch phrase to characterize a period of rapid change but as a descriptive designation of the process of transformation between what Engels called "two great and essentially different periods of economic history: the period of manufacture proper, based on the division of manual labor, and the period of modern industry based on machinery."[3] These are not, in Marx's view, two different social systems but rather two phases of capitalism.

Manufacture differs from handicraft production in its organization of the labor process, not in its basic methods and instruments. In handicraft production artisans produce saleable commodities and buy what they need (both consumption goods and means of production) from other similarly situated commodity producers. Division of labor within the workshop is severely limited by the fact that the master workman has at most a few journeymen and apprentices working with him. The guilds, with their strict rules and standards, gave appropriate institutional form to this mode of production and fought a long and bitter, though successful, battle to preserve its integrity.

The transition from handicraft production to capitalist manufacture was a part of the stormy process which Marx named "primitive accumulation."[4] It had two sides to it: the separation of a sizeable body of working people from their means of production, and the emergence of a group of persons with liquid wealth which they wished to put to profitable use. The uprooting of peasants through such measures as enclosures and the expropriation of Church lands created the necessary landless proletariat, while trade and plunder, given enormous impetus by the geographical discoveries of the late fifteenth and early sixteenth centuries, spawned an eager and willing capitalist class. The result was the emergence and spread of capitalist manufacture, at first largely in areas outside the jurisdiction of the guilds.

The methods and instruments of production in the new factories were essentially those of the artisan workshop; but now, owing to the larger number of workers involved and the complete domination of the production process by the capitalist, it became possible to subdivide the work and specialize the workers. The result was a tremendous increase in productivity due largely to the increased division of labor within the factory, a process that was so eloquently and lovingly described in Book I of *The Wealth of Nations*.

In Marx's view, an economic system based upon manufacture is essentially conservative. "History shows how the division of labor peculiar to manufacture, strictly so called, acquires the best adapted form at first by experience, as it were behind the backs of the actors, and then, like the guild handicrafts, strives to hold fast that form when once found, and here and there succeeds in keeping it for centuries."[5] But it is not only in this technological sense that such an economy is conservative. It also creates a highly differentiated labor force, dominated, numerically and otherwise, by skilled workers who tend to be contentious and undisciplined but incapable of sustained revolutionary activity. The economy and society based on manufacture is thus inherently change-resistant: it expands under the impact of capital accumulation but does not generate forces capable of altering its structure or, still less, of transforming it into something else.

It was this system that provided the model for classical political economy, which found its fullest and best known expression in Adam Smith's *The Wealth of Nations*. "What characterizes . . . him [Smith] as the political economist par excellence of the period of manufacture," Marx wrote, "is the stress he lays on the division of labor."[6] By comparison, Smith paid scant attention to machinery, so little, indeed, that Schumpeter felt justified in saying that with him "division of labor is practically the only factor in economic progress."[7] Nathan Rosenberg argues, persuasively I think, that Schumpeter's view needs qualification. Rosenberg holds that Smith recognized that the progress fostered by division of labor was limited to improvements within the existing technology and that major inventions are made not by workmen at all, or by capitalists either for that matter, but by "philosophers" who are totally separated from the productive process.[8] Nevertheless, as applied to Smith's economic theory proper, the point made by Schumpeter seems entirely valid: Smith allows for no dynamic force other than the division of labor. And Rosenberg's argument simply underscores the basically conservative character of that force.

Classical political economy reached its intellectual and scientific apex in the work of David Ricardo, and it was of course Ricardo who had the greatest influence on Marx. If Ricardo had shared Smith's interest in productive processes, it seems quite possible that he would have developed a different conception of the dynamics of capitalism; for in the four decades that separated *The Wealth of Nations* from the *Principles*, industrial technology advanced by giant strides. But Ricardo's interest was largely focused on the distribution of income among the major classes of capitalist society. What he had to say about the dynamics of the system was largely incidental.[9] In fact it is in the work of Ricardo that we find in its purest form the view of economic development "exclusively in terms of (gradual) quantitative changes in population, capital, wages, profits, and rent."[10]

Marx did share Smith's interest in productive processes, [11] and the reality which confronted him was so different from that which had confronted Smith nearly a century earlier that he could hardly help coming to radically different conclusions. Marx was certainly the first economist to develop a rounded conception of the industrial revolution and to take full account of its consequences in building his theoretical model of the capitalist process.[12]

We have already noted that for Marx the industrial revolution marked the transition between two essentially

different periods of capitalist development, the first being
characterized by the dominance of manufacture and the
second by the dominance of "modern industry." Although
quite aware that "epochs in the history of society are no
more separated from each other by hard and fast lines of
demarcation than are geological epochs,"[13] he nevertheless
found it useful to tie the industrial revolution to a specific
date.[14] By bringing out his spinning machine in 1735, John
Wyatt "began the industrial revolution of the 18th century."[15] In the nature of the case, no comparable date for
the end of the industrial revolution could be set, but we can
infer that Marx considered that the decisive structural change
in the system had been effected by the third decade of the
nineteenth century. This inference follows from (a) his view
that the business cycle is the unique and necessary attribute
of the modern-industry phase of capitalist development, and
(b) his dating of the first business cycle from the crisis of
1825.[16]

For Marx, the essence of the industrial revolution was the
replacement of handwork by machinery (*Capital,* I), a
process which takes place "from the moment that the tool
proper is taken from man and fitted into a mechanism" and
regardless of "whether the motive power is derived from man
or from some other machine" (p. 408). Once started in an
important part of the economy, this process of mechanization tends to spread in a series of chain reactions. As Marx put
it:

> A radical change in the mode of production in one
> sphere of industry involves a similar change in other
> spheres. This happens at first in such branches of
> industry as are connected together by being separate
> phases of a process, and yet are isolated by the social
> division of labor in such a way that each of them
> produces an independent commodity. Thus spinning by
> machinery made weaving by machinery a necessity, and

both together made the mechanical and chemical revolution that took place in bleaching, printing, and dyeing imperative. So too, on the other hand, the revolution in cotton spinning called forth the invention of the gin for separating the seeds from the cotton fiber; it was only by means of this invention that the production of cotton became possible on the enormous scale at present required. But more especially, the revolution in the modes of production of industry and agriculture made necessary a revolution in the general conditions of the social process of production, i.e., in the means of communication and transport. . . . Hence, apart from the radical changes introduced in the construction of sailing vessels, the means of communication and transport became gradually adapted to the modes of production of mechanical industry by the creation of a system of river steamers, railways, ocean steamers, and telegraphs. But the huge masses of iron that had now to be forged, to be welded, to be cut, to be bored, and to be shaped, demanded, on their part, cyclopean machines for the construction of which the methods of the manufacturing period were utterly inadequate.

Modern Industry had therefore itself to take in hand the machine, its characteristic instrument of production, and to construct machines by machines. It was not till it did this that it built up for itself a fitting technical foundation, and stood on its own feet. Machinery, simultaneously with the increasing use of it, in the first decades of this century, appropriated, by degrees, the fabrication of machines proper. But it was only during the decade preceding 1866 that the construction of railways and ocean steamers on a stupendous scale called into existence the cyclopean machines now employed in the construction of prime movers. [Pp. 418-20]

From this passage one could perhaps conclude that it was Marx's view that he was writing the first volume of *Capital* during the final stage of the transition from manufacture to modern industry. If he had had to pick out the single most important step forward in this whole vast movement, it would undoubtedly have been the perfection of the steam engine. Here again it is worthwhile to quote his own words:

> Not till the invention of Watt's second and so-called double-acting steam engine was a prime mover found, that begot its own force by the consumption of coal and water, that was mobile and a means of locomotion, that was urban and not, like the water-wheel, rural, that permitted production to be concentrated in towns instead of, like the water-wheels, being scattered up and down the country, that was of universal technical application, and, relatively speaking, little affected in its choice of residence by local circumstances. The greatness of Watt's genius showed itself in the specification of the patent that he took out in April, 1784. In that specification his steam engine is described, not as an invention for a specific purpose, but as an agent universally applicable in Mechanical Industry. In it he points out applications, many of which, as for instance the steam hammer, were not introduced until half a century later. [Pp. 411-12]

I cannot refrain from pointing out in passing the very striking similarity between the steam engine in the industrial revolution and the technology of automation in the radical transformation of production processes through which we are living in the second half of the twentieth century. "What the feedback and the vacuum tube have made possible," wrote the late Norbert Wiener, the father of cybernetics, "is not the sporadic design of individual automatic mechanisms, but a general policy for the construction of automatic mechanisms of the most varied type."[17] Here again we have a technological advance the importance of which stems not from its capacity to serve a specific purpose but from its universal applicability. And, as in the case of the steam engine, it seems certain that many of the applications will not be realized until many years later.[18]

To return to Marx's theory of the industrial revolution: Marx saw two respects in which an economy based on modern industry differs fundamentally from one based on manufacture. The first relates to the *modus operandi* of the production process itself; the second to the composition and nature of the working class. The net effect of these factors was to transform capitalism from a relatively conservative and change-resistant society into a super-dynamic society, headed, in Marx's view, for inevitable revolutionary overthrow.

With respect to the production process in modern industry, Marx held that technological progress ceases to depend on the ingenuity of the skilled laborer and/or the genius of the great inventor as it did in manufacture, and, instead, becomes the province of the rational sciences. A few quotations from the chapter on "Machinery and Modern Industry" (*Capital*, I) will show how explicit Marx was on this point and what enormous importance he attached to it:

> Intelligence in production . . . is lost by the detail laborers (and) is concentrated in the capital that employs them. . . . This separation . . . is completed in modern industry, which makes science a productive force distinct from labor and presses it into the service of capital. [Pp. 396-97]

> In Manufacture it is the workmen who, with their manual implements, must, either singly or in groups, carry on each particular detail process. If, on the one hand, the workman becomes adapted to the process, on the other, the process was previously made suitable to the workman. This subjective principle of the division of labor no longer exists in production by machinery. Here

the process as a whole is examined objectively, in itself, that is to say, without regard to the question of its execution by human hands, it is analyzed into its constituent phases; and the problem, how to execute each detail process and bind them all into a whole, is solved by the aid of machines, chemistry, etc. [Pp. 414-15]

The implements of labor, in the form of machinery, necessitate the substitution of natural forces for human force, and the conscious application of science instead of rule of thumb. In . . . its machinery system, Modern Industry has a productive organism that is purely objective, in which the laborer becomes a mere appendage to an already existing material condition of production. [P. 421]

When machinery is first introduced into an industry, new methods of reproducing it more cheaply follow blow upon blow, and so do improvements, that not only affect individual parts and details of the machine, but its entire build. [P. 442]

The principle, carried out in the factory system, of analyzing the process of production into its constituent phases, and of solving the problems thus proposed by the application of mechanics, of chemistry, and of the whole range of the natural sciences, becomes the determining principle everywhere. [P. 504]

Modern Industry rent the veil that concealed from men their own social process of production, and that turned the various, spontaneously divided branches of production into so many riddles, not only to outsiders but even to the initiated. The principle which it pursued of resolving each into its constituent movements without any regard to their possible execution by the hand of man, created the new modern science of technology.

The varied, apparently unconnected, and petrified forms of the production processes now resolved themselves into so many conscious and systematic applications of natural science to the attainment of given useful effects. Technology also discovered the few main fundamental forms of motion, which, despite the diversity of the instruments used, are necessarily taken by every productive action of the human body; just as the science of mechanics sees in the most complicated machinery nothing but the continual repetition of the simple mechanical powers. [P. 532]

Immediately following the last passage, Marx stated in its most explicit and succinct form the general conclusion which he deduced from these arguments:

Modern Industry never looks upon and treats the existing form of a process as final. The technical basis of that industry is therefore revolutionary, while all earlier modes of production were essentially conservative.[19] By means of machinery, chemical processes, and other methods, it is continually causing changes not only in the technical basis of production, but also in the functions of the laborer and the labor-process.[20]

Marx's theory of the effects of machinery on the working class is certainly among his best-known doctrines and need not be reviewed in any detail here. His central thesis, from which the rest followed quite logically, was that machinery does away with, or at any rate drastically reduces, the need for special skills and instead puts a premium on quickness and dexterity. It thereby opens the door to the mass employment of women and children and cheapens the labor power of adult males by obviating the need for long and expensive training programs. There follows a vast expansion of the labor supply which is augmented and supplemented by two further factors: (a) once solidly entrenched in the basic industries, machinery invades ever new branches of the economy, underselling the old handworkers and casting them onto the labor market, and (b) the progressive improvement of machinery in industries already conquered continuously eliminates existing jobs and reduces the employment-creating power of a given rate of capital accumulation. The effects of machinery are thus, on the one hand, to expand, homogenize, and reduce the costs of production of the labor force; and, on the other hand, to slow down the rate of increase of the demand for labor. This means a sea-change in the economic power relation between capital and labor, to the enormous advantage of the former. Wages are driven down to, and often below, the barest subsistence minimum; hours of work are increased beyond anything known before; intensity of labor is stepped up to match the ever increasing speed of the machinery. Machinery thus completes the process of subjecting labor to the sway of capital that was begun in the period of primitive accumulation. It is the capitalistic employment of machinery, and not merely capitalism in general, which generates the modern proletariat as Marx conceived it.

But there are no medals without two sides. Economically, the power of the proletariat under modern industry is much reduced compared to that of its predecessor in the period of manufacture. But politically, its potential power is infinitely greater. Old geographical and craft divisions and jealousies are eliminated or minimized. The nature of work in the modern factory requires the organization and disciplining of the workers, thereby preparing them for organized and disciplined action in other fields. The extreme of exploitation to which they are subjected deprives them of any interest in the existing social order, forces them to live in conditions in which morality is meaningless and family life impossible, and ends by totally alienating them from their work, their products, their society, and even themselves. Unlike their predecessors in the period of manufacture, these workers form a proletariat which is both capable of, and has every interest in, revolutionary action to overthrow the existing social order. They are the ones of whom Marx and Engels had already said in the *Communist Manifesto:* "The proletarians have nothing to lose but their chains. They have a world to win." In *Capital* this bold generalization is supported by a painstaking analysis of the immanent characteristics and tendencies of capitalistic "modern industry" as it emerged from the industrial revolution.

In this paper I have tried to explain the difference between the theory of capitalist development of the classics and that of Marx as being due, at least in part, to the fact that the former took as their model an economy based on manufacture, which is an essentially conservative and change-resistant economic order; while Marx, recognizing and making full allowance for the profound transformation effected by the industrial revolution, took as his model an economy based on modern machine industry, which is certainly highly dynamic and which Marx himself thought was headed for inevitable revolution. In conclusion, I should like to add a few remarks contrasting Marx's treatment of technological change with that of post-classical bourgeois economics and assessing the validity—or perhaps it would be better to say the fruitlessness—of his views on the implications of machinery for the functioning and future of the capitalist system.

While Marx put technological change at the very center of economic theory, it is hardly an exaggeration to say that the bourgeois successors of classical political economy—the marginalists of various countries and schools—banished it altogether. Consumption rather than production became the starting point of economic theorizing, and its adepts concerned themselves more and more with tendencies to equilibrium and less and less with the macrodynamics of the system as a whole. This of course did not happen all at once or completely: men like Marshall and Taussig, for example, were very much interested in methods of production or, to use a term which was current around the turn of the century, the state of the industrial arts. But their interest was akin to that of the historian, the intelligent observer, the educated man—it was not vitally related to their economic theory. And later on, as economists became increasingly specialized and decreasingly educated, interest in real production was progressively replaced by interest in imaginary "production functions."

There was one great exception among bourgeois economists, one outstanding figure who sought, under the influence of Marx and in opposition to the Marxists, to establish a rival theory of economic development centering on technological change. I refer of course to Joseph Schumpeter, whose *Theory of Economic Development* was first published (in German) in 1912. A detailed comparison of the theories of Schumpeter and Marx would certainly be a useful project but one which obviously cannot be undertaken within the scope of the present essay. I will content myself with observing that Schumpeter's treatment of technological change departed from Marx's on an issue that Marx considered to be of decisive importance, namely, the objective character of the process. For Marx, once machinery had taken firm hold it was bound to spread, to evolve into progressively more elaborate and productive forms, to harness all the natural sciences to its imperatives—and all this quite apart from the desires or intentions of individual capitalists or scientists.[21] For Schumpeter, on the other hand, technological change is essentially a by-product of the spontaneous innovating activity of individual entrepreneurs. There is no need for us, living in the second half of the twentieth century, to pass judgment on this theory: history has already done so. The interconnection between science, technology, and production was largely informal and unstructured a hundred years ago;

since then, and especially during and after the Second World War, it has become ever closer, more institutionalized, more deliberately planned. Without denying that individual inventors and entrepreneurs still play a role in the process of technological change, we surely cannot compare their importance to that of the great government- and industry-financed laboratories where the bulk of research and development in today's advanced technologies takes place.

Schumpeter himself saw this coming as long ago as the 1920s, and in his book, *Capitalism, Socialism and Democracy,* he included a section ("The Obsolescence of the Entrepreneurial Function") in which he virtually abandoned his old theory of innovation. "Technological progress," he wrote, "is increasingly becoming the business of teams of trained specialists who turn out what is required and make it work in predictable ways."[22]

Nothing in Schumpeter's original theory of economic development could have led us to expect this outcome. But, from the point of view of Marx's theory of the objectivization of the process of technological progress and the harnessing of science to its requirements, it is precisely the outcome which is most logical and natural. Indeed, what must strike one today as one re-reads Marx's chapter on "Machinery and Modern Industry" in the light of recent history is its modernity, its direct relevance to what is happening under our very eyes. One is even tempted to assume that much of what Marx wrote on the subject a hundred years ago was more prophetic than literally true of mid-nineteenth-century Britain.

The same cannot be said about Marx's analysis of the effects of machinery on the working class. The trends which he stressed and projected into the future—flooding of the labor market by women and children, homogenization of the labor force, abasement of living standards and conditions, etc.—reached their maximum intensity in the first half of the nineteenth century and had already been checked or reversed before the publication of the first volume of *Capital*. There were many factors at work here. One was state action, resulting partly from the political struggles of the working class itself and partly from the interest of the bourgeoisie in a healthier and better-trained labor force. Another was the growing strength of trade unions. And still another was the expansion of what is nowadays called the service sector of the economy, an expansion made possible by, and sustained from, the rising surplus product associated with the progressive mechanization of production.

Marx's failure was not that he did not recognize the existence of these counteracting forces. In the case of state action, he provided a detailed analysis of legislation regulating the length of the working day and of the factory acts; and the principles underlying this analysis could easily be extended to apply to other forms of social welfare legislation. And in various passages scattered throughout his writings he showed that he was well aware not only of the importance of trade unions as weapons in the working class struggle but also of the proliferation of what he, following the classics, called the "unproductive" occupations. Marx's failure was rather in not understanding that all these counteracting forces taken together could actually come to prevail and thus turn a potentially revolutionary proletariat into an actual reformist force.

But we must also note another failure of Marx which cuts in a rather different direction. He saw very clearly the most striking international consequence of the industrial revolution:

> So soon . . . as the general conditions requisite for production by the modern industrial system have been established, this mode of production acquires an elasticity, a capacity for sudden extension by leaps and bounds that finds no hindrance except in the supply of

raw material and in the disposal of the produce. On the one hand, the immediate effect of machinery is to increase the supply of raw material in the same way, for example, as the cotton gin augmented the production of cotton. On the other hand, the cheapness of the articles produced by machinery, and the improved means of transport and communication furnish the weapons for conquering foreign markets. By ruining handicraft production in other countries, machinery forcibly converts them into fields for the supply of its raw material. In this way East India was compelled to produce cotton, wool, hemp, jute, and indigo for Great Britain. . . . A new and international division of labor, a division suited to the requirements of the chief centers of modern industry springs up, and converts one part of the globe into a chiefly agricultural field of production for supplying the other part which remains a chiefly industrial field.[23]

What Marx did not foresee was that this "new and international division of labor" might harden into a pattern of development and underdevelopment which would split mankind into haves and have-nots on a scale far wider and deeper than the bourgeois/proletarian split in the advanced capitalist countries themselves. If Marx had foreseen this momentous development, he could have easily conceded the existence of meliorative trends within the advanced countries without for a moment giving up the prediction of inevitable revolutionary overthrow for the system as a whole.

Notes:

1. *The Theory of Capitalist Development* (New York: Monthly Review Press, 1953), p. 94; originally published in 1942 by Oxford University Press.

2. See especially the first section of Marx's chapter on "Machinery and Modern Industry," *Capital*, I, pp. 405-522.

3. Editor's "Preface to the First English Translation," ibid., p. 29.

4. The German is *ursprüngliche Akkumulation*, which literally means "original accumulation," and in this case the literal translation would have been better since what Marx wanted to convey was that this kind of accumulation preceded capitalist accumulation proper. "Primitive accumulation," however, is the generally accepted translation and to change it is to risk being misunderstood.

5. Marx, *Capital*, I, p. 399.

6. Ibid., p. 383n.

7. Schumpeter, *History of Economic Analysis*, p. 187.

8. Nathan Rosenberg, "Adam Smith on the Division of Labour: Two Views or One?" *Economica*, XXXII (May 1965), p. 128.

9. David Ricardo's chapter "On Machinery" was tacked onto the third edition of the *Principles* and was concerned entirely with the question of whether it was possible for machinery to displace labor. In the course of this analysis, he stated that "with every augmentation of capital, a greater proportion of it is employed on machinery" and that the demand for labor "will continue to increase with an increase in capital, but not in proportion to its increase; the ratio will, necessarily, be a diminishing ratio" (*Principles of Political Economy and Taxation*, Everyman's ed. [New York: E. P. Dutton and Co., 1933], p. 387). These propositions could have formed the starting point of a fruitful line of analysis, but with Ricardo they remained hardly more than *obiter dicta*. It was left for Marx to explore their implications.

10. Ricardo, *Principles*, p. 107.

11. In his biography of Marx, Mehring tells of an incident in which a manufacturer remarked that Marx too must have been a manufacturer at some time. Marx's reply (in a letter to Engels) was: "If people only knew how little I know about all this business!" Franz Mehring, *Karl Marx: The Story of His Life* (New York: Covici, 1935), p. 285.

12. I am tempted to say that the whole idea of the industrial revolution, which in my student days was commonly associated with the name of the elder Toynbee, really originated with Marx. But I confess that I do not know the relevant literature well enough to be sure.

13. Marx, *Capital*, I, p. 405.
14. Similarly the recognition that "a critical history of technology would show how little any of the inventions of the eighteenth century are the work of a single individual" (ibid., p. 406) did not prevent him from associating inventions with the names of individuals.
15. Ibid.
16. Speaking of the period 1820 to 1830 in the Preface to the second edition of Volume I of *Capital*, Marx wrote that "modern industry itself was only just emerging from the age of childhood, as is shown by the fact that with the crisis of 1825 it for the first time opens the periodic cycle of its modern life" (ibid., p. 18).
17. Norbert Wiener, *The Human Use of Human Beings: Cybernetics and Society* (Boston: Houghton Mifflin, 1954), p. 179.
18. Should the current technological transformation of the process of production, in which automation unquestionably plays a decisive role, be called a new industrial revolution? In purely technological terms it is doubtless as radical and thoroughgoing as the industrial revolution of the eighteenth and nineteenth centuries. And yet to a Marxist, at any rate, the appropriateness of the designation must seem at least doubtful. Capitalism has entered a new phase since Marx's day, the phase of monopoly capitalism. In technological terms, however, as Marx well understood, this transition was but the logical consequence of trends inherent in the very modern industry which he described and analyzed in *Capital* ("concentration" and "centralization" of capital: see Marx, *Capital*, I, especially pp. 685-89). It has yet to be shown that the current technological transformation is introducing yet another phase of capitalist development. Unless this can be shown, it seems to me that the use of the term "revolution" to describe what is now taking place can only lead to confusion.
19. In order to drive home the point still further and to extend the scope of its significance, Marx here adds a footnote quoting a famous passage from the *Communist Manifesto:*

    "The bourgeoisie cannot exist without continually revolutionizing the instruments of production, and thereby the relations of production and all the social relations. Conservation, in an unaltered form, of the old modes of production was on the contrary the first condition of existence for all earlier industrial classes. Constant revolution in production, uninterrupted disturbance of all social conditions, everlasting uncertainty and agitation, distinguish the bourgeois epoch from all earlier ones. All fixed fast-frozen relations, with their train of ancient and venerable prejudices and opinions, are swept away, all new formed ones become antiquated before they can ossify. All that is solid melts into air, all that is holy is profaned, and man is at last compelled to face with sober senses his real conditions of life, and his relations with his kind."

If, in the *Manifesto*, this can be said to have had the character of a brilliant insight, the corresponding but less sweeping passage in *Capital* has the character of a reasoned deduction from an exhaustive study of the actual processes of production prevailing in England in the middle of the nineteenth century.

20. Marx, *Capital*, I, pp. 532-33.

21. The *objectivity* of technique and technological advance must not be confused with the *supremacy* of technique as preached for example by the Frenchman Jacques Ellul (*The Technological Society* [New York: Alfred A. Knopf, 1964]). Technique does not operate and advance independently of the social framework but only independently of the will of individuals within the social framework. Ellul's book is a wonderful demonstration of what nonsense can result from failing to make this crucial distinction.

22. Schumpeter, *Capitalism, Socialism and Democracy*, p. 132.

23. Marx, *Capital*, I, pp. 492-93.

Marx and the
Proletariat

Marx's theory of capitalism, which was sketched with broad and sweeping strokes in the *Communist Manifesto* and achieved its most comprehensive and polished form in the first volume of *Capital,* published just a hundred years ago, holds that capitalism is a self-contradictory system which generates increasingly severe difficulties and crises as it develops. But this is only half the story: equally characteristic of capitalism is that it generates not only difficulties and crises but also its own gravediggers in the shape of the modern proletariat. A social system can be ever so self-contradictory and still be without a revolutionary potential: the outcome can be, and in fact history shows many examples where it has been, stagnation, misery, starvation, subjugation by a stronger and more vigorous society. In Marx's view capitalism was not such a society; it was headed not for slow death or subjugation but for a thoroughgoing revolutionary transformation. And the reason was precisely because by its

This is the text of a paper delivered at the Third Annual Socialist Scholars Conference held in New York on September 9-10, 1967. It also appeared in the December 1967 issue of *Monthly Review.*

very nature it had to produce the agent which would revolutionize it. This is the crucially important role which the proletariat plays in the Marxian theoretical schema.

In the eyes of many people, including not a few who consider themselves to be essentially Marxists, this theory of the revolutionary agency of the proletariat is the weakest point of the whole system. They point to the fact that the English and other Western European proletariats, which Marx considered to be the vanguard of the international revolutionary movement, have actually developed into reformist forces which, by accepting the basic assumptions of capitalism, in fact strengthen it. And they note that the proletariat of what has become the most advanced and powerful capitalist country, the United States of America, has never developed a significant revolutionary leadership or movement, and shows fewer signs of doing so today than at any time in its history.

I do not believe that the empirical observations which support this type of criticism of Marx's theory can be seriously challenged. And yet it certainly will not do to jump from there to the conclusion that Marx's theory is "refuted" and must be abandoned. A more legitimate procedure, I suggest, is to inquire into the inner logic of the theory to discover *why* Marx assigned the role of revolutionary agent to the proletariat. In this way I believe we shall find that it is not the theory itself which is at fault so much as its misinterpretation and misapplication.

First, we must be quite clear that Marx's theory of the revolutionary agency of the proletariat has nothing to do with an emotional attachment to, or blind faith in, the working class as such. He believed that objective forces, generated by the capitalist system, were inexorably molding a revolutionary class, i.e., one which would have both the ability and the will to overthrow the existing order. The ability stemmed from its numerical strength and its indispensable role in the capitalist production process, the will from its being deprived not only of material possessions but of its essential and ultimately irrepressible humanity. Marx's position is perhaps most clearly stated in the following passage from *The Holy Family:*

When socialist writers ascribe this world-historical role to the proletariat, this is not at all . . . because they take the proletarians for gods. Quite the contrary. Because the abstraction of all humanity, even the appearance of humanity, is practically complete in the fully developed proletariat, because the living conditions of the proletariat represent the focal point of all inhuman conditions in contemporary society, because the human being is lost in the proletariat, but has won a theoretical consciousness of loss and is compelled by unavoidable and absolutely compulsory need (the practical expression of necessity) to revolt against this inhumanity—all these are the reasons why the proletariat can and must emancipate itself. However, it cannot emancipate itself without abolishing the conditions which give it life, and it cannot abolish these conditions without abolishing all those inhuman conditions of social life which are summed up in its own situation.

It does not go through the hard and hardening school of labor fruitlessly. It is not a question of what this or that proletarian, or even the proletariat as a whole, may imagine for the moment to be the aim. It is a question of what the proletariat actually is and what it will be compelled to do historically as the result of this being. The aim and the historical action of the proletariat are laid down in advance, irrevocably and obviously, in its own situation in life and in the whole organization of contemporary bourgeois society.[1]

The next question is this: What were the processes which molded a proletariat with these particular characteristics? One answer, which I suppose many Marxists would subscribe to, would hold that the revolutionary proletariat is inherent in capitalism and is therefore the creation of the very same processes which originally brought the system into existence and which have subsequently propelled its development. The first step, in this view, was what Marx called primitive accumulation which in one aspect was essentially the violent and bloody process of separating the working people from ownership of their means of production. After that, the expansion of the proletariat to its ultimate position of numerical dominance in capitalist society was the natural result of expanded reproduction on a capitalist basis. Expanded reproduction, as you know, consists of the appropriation by capitalists of surplus value created by wage laborers, and the continuous conversion of part of the surplus value into additional capital.

Now there can be no question that this is an accurate account of Marx's theory of the birth and *quantitative* expansion of the proletariat. But does it explain why he regarded the proletariat as the revolutionary agent destined to overthrow the system? If we say that it does, we necessarily imply that the proletariat was revolutionary from its birth and that only quantitative predominance was required for it to be able to perform its revolutionary function; for there is nothing in the mere mechanics of the expanded reproduction process to bring about a *qualitative* transformation of the proletariat. At this point it is therefore of first importance to recognize that in Marx's view the proletariat was *not* a revolutionary force from its birth but on the contrary acquired this quality in the course of its capitalistic development.

In this connection it is necessary to recall an aspect of Marx's theory of capitalism which is of course known to all students of the subject but which, I believe, is generally considered to have mostly historical interest. This is his division of the capitalist epoch into what Engels, in his editor's preface to the first English edition of the first volume of *Capital*, called "two great and essentially different periods of economic history: the period of manufacture proper, based on the division of manual labor, and the period of modern industry based on machinery." What separated the two periods was the industrial revolution, a term much used by Marx, the beginning of which he dated from Wyatt's spinning machine of 1735, and which had worked its transforming effects by 1825, a year of economic crisis in which "modern industry . . . for the first time opens the periodic cycle of its modern life."[2]

From our present point of view there are two fundamental differences between these phases of capitalist development. One relates to the dynamics of the production process itself, the other to the changed character of the proletariat brought about by the transition from the earlier phase to the later. (It should be noted in passing that the formal concepts of Marxian economic theory—constant and variable capital, surplus value, expanded reproduction, etc.—are equally applicable to both phases. At the level of abstraction implied by this conceptual apparatus, there is therefore no difference between the two phases, which is perhaps why many Marxist economists have failed to appreciate the importance of distinguishing between them.)

Manufacture is an extension and adaptation of age-old handicraft methods of production. The chief innovation is the assembling of many craftsmen in a single enterprise, which permits forms and degrees of specialization unthinkable under the medieval guild system. This specialization of crafts—or division of labor, as it was called by Adam Smith, the theorist *par excellence* of the manufacture phase—results in an enormous increase in labor productivity and in this sense marks a great stride forward in human progress. However, it is important to recognize that, technologically, manufacture is still an essentially conservative mode of production. The increase of productivity for which it is responsible stems from the more rational utilization of existing technologies, not from the introduction of new technologies. The latter process, often called invention, is no part of the logic of manufacture. Hence, in Marx's words: "History shows how the division of labor peculiar to manufacture, strictly so called, acquires the best adapted form at first by experience, as it were behind the backs of the actors, and then, like the guild handicrafts, strives to hold fast that form when once found, and here and there succeeds in keeping it for centuries" (p. 399). This naturally does not mean that invention was absent or that the culture and ideology of this phase of capitalism did not favor the inventive arts. If such had been the case, there would have been no industrial revolution at the time and in the place where it actually occurred. What it does mean is that invention was not an integral part of the process of production and indeed was often strongly resisted by the practitioners of existing methods of production. This special combination of circumstances, both favoring and inhibiting the progress of invention, found an interesting reflection in Adam Smith who, as Nathan Rosenberg has shown,[3] regarded major inventions as the work of neither laborers nor capitalists but rather of "philosophers" who are totally separated from the productive process.

The labor force of the manufacturing phase corresponded to the requirements of this particular mode of production. It consisted of a multitude of craftsmen possessing a great variety of specialized skills which were characteristically passed on from father to son. Craft consciousness rather than class consciousness was the hallmark of a proletariat so composed. The skilled handworker tended to be bigoted, proud, undisciplined, contentious, capable of waging a bitter and often violent struggle against the constraints of capitalist production and the employer who imposed them upon him. But his vision was necessarily limited: he could not see the system as a whole nor understand his place in it, and he was therefore incapable of sustained revolutionary activity to change it. Capitalism in its manufacturing phase, in addition to being technologically conservative was also highly resistant to political and social change.

The introduction of machinery—which, according to Marx, takes place "from the moment that the tool proper is taken from man and fitted into a mechanism" (p. 408)—changed all that. Having once occurred in one important branch of industry, it literally forced itself on other branches until it finally came to dominate the mode of production as a whole. Marx's account of this process is worth quoting at some length:

> A radical change in the mode of production in one sphere of industry involves a similar change in other spheres. This happens at first in such branches of industry as are connected together by being separate phases of a process, and yet are isolated by the social division of labor in such a way that each of them produces an independent commodity. Thus spinning by machinery made weaving by machinery a necessity, and both together made the mechanical and chemical revolution that took place in bleaching, printing, and dyeing imperative. So too, on the other hand, the revolution in cotton spinning called forth the invention of the gin for separating the seeds from the cotton fibre; it was only by means of this invention that the production of cotton became possible on the enormous scale at present required. But more especially, the revolution in the modes of production of industry and agriculture made necessary a revolution in the general conditions of the social process of production, i.e., in the means of communication and transport. Hence, apart from the radical changes introduced in the construction of sailing vessels, the means of communication and transport became gradually adapted to the modes of production of mechanical industry by the

creation of a system of river steamers, railways, ocean steamers, and telegraphs. But the huge masses of iron that had now to be forged, to be welded, to be cut, to be bored, and to be shaped, demanded, on their part, cyclopean machines for the construction of which the methods of the manufacturing period were utterly inadequate.

Modern industry had therefore itself to take in hand the machine, its characteristic instrument of production, and to construct machines by machines. It was not till it did this that it built up for itself a fitting technical foundation, and stood on its own feet. Machinery, simultaneously with the increasing use of it, in the first decades of this century appropriated, by degrees, the fabrication of machines proper. But it was only during the decade preceding 1866 that the construction of railways and ocean steamers on a stupendous scale called into existence the cyclopean machines now employed in the construction of prime movers. [Pp. 418-20]

Whereas capitalism in its manufacturing phase was technologically conservative and immune to the threat of revolutionary change, modern industry based on machinery is the opposite in both respects. Technological progress no longer depends on the ingenuity of the skilled worker or on the genius of the great inventor; it now becomes the province of the rational sciences. This is one of the major themes of Marx's masterful chapter entitled "Machinery and Modern Industry" which alone would be enough to mark the first volume of *Capital* as an epoch-making work. Here we must be content with a couple of brief quotations which convey the gist of his thought:

The principle, carried out in the factory system, of analyzing the process of production into its constituent phases, and of solving the problems thus proposed by the application of mechanics, of chemistry, and of the whole range of the natural sciences, becomes the determining principle everywhere. [P. 504]

Modern Industry rent the veil that concealed from men their own social process of production, and that turned various spontaneously divided branches of production into so many riddles, not only to outsiders but even to the initiated. The principle which it pursued of resolving each into its constituent parts without any regard to their possible execution by the hand of man, created the new modern science of technology. The varied, apparently unconnected, and petrified forms of the production process now resolved themselves into so many conscious and systematic applications of natural science to the attainment of given useful effects. [P. 532]

From this the conclusion flowed logically: "Modern Industry never looks upon and treats the existing form of a process as final. The technical base of that industry is therefore revolutionary, while all earlier modes of production were essentially conservative" (p. 532).

With respect to its social base, Marx regarded modern industrial capitalism as no less revolutionary—once again in sharp contrast to capitalism in its manufacturing phase. Machinery progressively abolishes the crafts which are the basis of manufacture and thereby renders obsolete the multitudinous special skills of the craftsmen. In this way it cheapens the labor power of adult males by obviating the need for prolonged and expensive training programs. At the same time, by putting a premium on dexterity and quickness it opens the door to the mass employment of women and children. There followed a vast expansion of the labor supply which was augmented and supplemented by two further factors: (a) once solidly entrenched in the basic industries, machinery invades ever new branches of the economy, undercutting the old handworkers and casting them onto the labor market; and (b) the progressive improvement of machinery in industries already conquered continuously eliminates existing jobs and reduces the employment-creating power of a given rate of capital accumulation.

The effects of machinery, in short, are on the one hand to extend, homogenize, and reduce the costs of production of the labor force; on the other, to slow down the rate of increase of the demand for labor power. This means a fundamental change in the economic power relation between capital and labor, to the enormous advantage of the former. Wages are driven down to, and often below, the barest subsistence minimum; hours of work are increased beyond anything known before; the intensity of labor is stepped up to match the ever increasing speed of the machinery. Machinery thus completes the process, begun in the period of primitive accumulation, of subjecting labor to the sway of capital. It is the capitalistic employment of machinery, and not merely capitalism in general, which generates the modern proletariat as Marx conceived it.

But the coin has two sides. Economically, the power of the proletariat under modern industry is much reduced compared to that of its predecessor in the period of manufacture. But politically, its potential power is infinitely greater. Old craft and geographical divisions and jealousies are eliminated or minimized. The nature of work in the modern factory requires the organization and disciplining of the workers, thereby preparing them for organized and disciplined action in other fields. The extreme of exploitation to which they are subjected deprives them of any interest in the existing social order, forces them to live in conditions in which morality is meaningless and family life impossible, and ends by totally alienating them from their work, their products, their society, and even themselves. Unlike the skilled craftsmen of the period of manufacture, these workers form a proletariat which is both capable of, and has every interest in, revolutionary action to overthrow the existing social order.

These are the ones of whom Marx and Engels had already declared in the *Communist Manifesto:* "The proletarians have nothing to lose but their chains. They have a world to win." In the first volume of *Capital* this bold generalization is supported by a painstaking analysis of the immanent features and tendencies of capitalist "modern industry" as it emerged from the industrial revolution.

So far I have tried to show that Marx's theory of capitalism encompasses two quite distinct phases, separated by the industrial revolution, which can be characterized as follows:

Manufacture

| Technology | Conservative |
| Proletariat | Nonrevolutionary |

Modern Industry

| Technology | Revolutionary |
| Proletariat | Revolutionary |

It must be immediately added, however, that the word "revolutionary" applied to technology has a somewhat different meaning from what it does when applied to the proletariat. A revolutionary technology is one which by its very nature changes continuously and rapidly; a revolutionary proletariat, on the other hand, is one which has the *potential* to make a revolution but which can actually make it only once under favorable conditions (the so-called revolutionary situation). Here a question obviously arises: if, for whatever reason, the emergence of a revolutionary situation is long delayed, what will be the effect in the meantime of modern industry's revolutionary technology on the composition and capabilities of the proletariat?

Marx never asked this question, perhaps because it never occurred to him that the revolution might be long delayed. And yet it is a question which arises quite naturally within the framework of his theory. He had explicitly recognized that modern industry "is continually causing changes not only in the technical basis of production, but also in the functions of the laborer and in the labor process" (p. 533); and no one knew better than he that it is the functions of the laborer and the nature of the labor process which determine the character of the proletariat. In the absence of a revolutionary situation, would the proletariat tend to become more or less revolutionary? It would have been a perfectly logical question for Marx to ask when he was writing *Capital*; a hundred years later it seems to be not only a logical but an inescapable question for Marx's followers.

This is obviously not the occasion to attempt a comprehensive answer, and I have to admit that my knowledge of the interrelation between technology and the labor process is far too limited to permit me to speak as an expert on the subject. I will therefore restrict myself to indicating in a very general way why it seems to me that the advance of modern technology must tend to shape a proletariat which is less rather than more revolutionary that that which emerged from the industrial revolution in the middle of the nineteenth century.

I would not put the main emphasis on the consequences of technological change for the workers who actually mind the machines and do functionally similar work, much of it virtually unknown in Marx's time, such as manning assembly lines. These are still for the most part dehumanizing jobs requiring little skill; and speed-up of machinery and increasing work loads certainly do not make them more bearable, not to say attractive. A proletariat dominated by operatives of this general description might well have as great a revolutionary potential as its mid-nineteenth-century predecessor. The point is that relative to the total work force there are so many fewer jobs of this kind than there used to be. Progressive mechanization of particular processes, and more recently the perfection of generally applicable methods of partial or full automation, have reduced this traditional blue-collar segment of the proletariat from what was once a large majority to what is today in the most industrialized societies a small minority. Since the output of this minority has at the same time enormously increased, it is clear that modern technology has multiplied the productivity of labor many times over and put within society's grasp a potential surplus of vast proportions.

The obverse of this development is that a great variety of new categories of jobs has been created. Some of these are integrally related to the new technology—scientists, researchers, engineers, technicians, highly skilled maintenance and repair men, etc.—but many more (both absolutely and relatively) are concerned in one way or another with the manipulation and absorption of the surplus made possible by the increased productivity of the underlying production workers. Under this heading one could list government workers of all kinds, including teachers; those employed in the many branches of the sales apparatus, including most of the personnel of the mass communications media; workers and salaried personnel in finance, insurance, and real estate; and the providers of many different kinds of personal services from beauty treatment to sports spectacles. In the United States today these job categories, taken all together, probably account for close to three-quarters of the employed nonagricultural labor force.

In terms of the occupational composition of the labor force, then, the two chief consequences of modern industry's revolutionary technology have been (a) a drastic (and continuing) reduction in the production-worker component, and (b) a vast proliferation of job categories in the distribution and service sectors of the economy. At the same time there has taken place a slow but cumulatively substantial increase in the real wages of both production and nonproduction workers. In part this reflects an increase in the cost of production of labor power as the educational and training requirements of the new employment categories have risen. And in part it reflects the fact that the workers—and here we mean primarily production workers—have been able through nonrevolutionary class struggle to wrest from the capitalists a part of the fruits of increasing productivity.

To sum up: The revolutionary technology of modern industry, correctly described and analyzed by Marx,[4] has had the effect of multiplying by many times the productivity of basic production workers. This in turn has resulted in a sharp reduction in their relative importance in the labor force, in the proliferation of new job categories, and in a gradually rising standard of living for employed workers. In short, the first effects of the introduction of machinery—expansion and homogenization of the labor force and reduction in the costs of production (value) or labor power—have been largely reversed. Once again, as in the period of manufacture, the proletariat is highly differentiated; and once again occupational and status consciousness has tended to submerge class consciousness.

It might be thought that despite these changes the blue-collar proletariat would remain a revolutionary element within the working class as a whole. No doubt there is a tendency for this to happen, and it would be shortsighted in the extreme to overlook the revolutionary potential still remaining in this large body of workers. But one must not go too far in isolating them from the rest of the labor force. As James Boggs says:

> Today most workers in the plant [i.e., blue-collar workers] have been to high school and quite a few have even been to college. All either plan or wish to send their sons and daughters to college—their sons so they won't have to work in the factory on what they call a dull and automated job; their daughters . . . so they won't have to marry some bum but can make their own living and be free to decide whether they want to marry or not marry. . . .[5]

In other words, blue-collar workers, being a diminishing

minority of the whole working class, do not think of their families as permanently stuck in the stratum which they occupy. As long as this is so, their attitudes and ideology are not likely to be radically different from those of the nonrevolutionary majority of the working class which surrounds them.

If we accept these general propositions about the direct and indirect effects of modern technology on the composition and character of the working class, must we conclude that Marx's theory of the proletariat has been refuted? I do not think so. His theory in fact dealt with the early impact of machinery on the proletariat, not with the longer-run consequences of the machine technology for the proletariat. One might perhaps complain that Marx did not attempt to develop a more comprehensive theory; and one could argue, I think persuasively, that he certainly could have done so. Indeed, from many remarks scattered throughout his writings, it would probably be possible for a follower of Marx to construct a more or less systematic theory of what the future held in store for the proletariat if capitalism should survive the revolutionary threat inherent in the early period of modern industry. But this is not the occasion for such an effort, and the fact that Marx himself did not make it provides no justification for denying the validity of the theory he did put forward within the limits of its applicability.

In this connection I would go further and argue that the Russian Revolution of 1917 provides extremely strong empirical evidence for the validity of Marx's theory. This revolution occurred in a capitalist country where modern industry was in the process of establishing itself and where it had already created a large and highly revolutionary urban proletariat. Under these circumstances, when the revolutionary situation matured (as it had not done in the Western European countries at a comparable stage of development), the proletariat played precisely the role attributed to it in

Marx's theory. In the social sciences, a theory rarely receives a more striking confirmation.

Here, however, a much more serious question arises: does the fact that capitalism in Western Europe and North America survived the initial period of modern industry and that its new technology then went on progressively to reduce the revolutionary potential of the proletariat, mean that as of the second half of the twentieth century we have to abandon the whole idea of a revolutionary agent destined to overthrow the capitalist order? Again, I do not think so.

The belief that the *industrial* proletariat is the only possible revolutionary agent under capitalism stems from focusing attention too exclusively on the advanced capitalist countries where modern industry got its start and where the new technology has had a chance to develop under favorable conditions. But capitalism as a social order has never consisted only of industrialized countries. In fact, as Marx explicitly recognized, the industrialization of some countries had as its counterpart from the outset the nonindustrialization of others, with the two sets of countries being integrally tied together in a single system.

> So soon ... as the general conditions requisite for production by the modern industrial system have been established, this mode of production acquires an elasticity, a capacity for sudden extension by leaps and bounds that finds no hindrance except in the supply of raw material and in the disposal of the produce. On the one hand, the immediate effect of machinery is to increase the supply of raw material in the same way, for example, as the cotton gin augmented the production of cotton. On the other hand, the cheapness of the articles produced by the machinery, and the improved means of transport and communications furnish the weapons for conquering foreign markets. By ruining handicraft production in other countries, machinery forcibly converts them into fields for the supply of its raw material. In

this way East India was compelled to produce cotton, wool, hemp, jute, and indigo for Great Britain. . . . A new and international division of labor, a division suited to the requirements of the chief centers of modern industry springs up, and converts one part of the globe into a chiefly agricultural field of production for supplying the other part which remains a chiefly industrial field. [Pp. 492-93]

Once it is recognized that capitalism is not and never has been confined to one or more industrializing countries, but is rather a global system embracing both the (relatively few) industrializing countries and their (relatively numerous) satellites and dependencies, it becomes quite clear that the future of the system cannot be adequately analyzed in terms of the forces at work in any part of the system but must take full account of the *modus operandi* of the system as a whole.

Lenin was the first Marxist to see this and to begin work on the theoretical extensions and reformulations which it made necessary. His major contribution was his little book *Imperialism: the Highest Stage of Capitalism* which, having been published in 1917, is exactly half as old as the first volume of *Capital.* There he argued that "Capitalism has grown into a world system of colonial oppression and of the financial strangulation of the overwhelming majority of the people of the world by a handful of 'advanced' countries. And this 'booty' is shared between two or three powerful world pirates armed to the teeth. . . ." He also argued that the capitalists of the imperialist countries could and do use a part of their "booty" to bribe and win over to their side an aristocracy of labor. As far as the logic of the argument is concerned, it could be extended to a majority or even all the workers in the industrialized countries. In any case, it is clear that taking account of the global character of the capitalist system provides strong additional reasons for believing that the tendency in this stage of capitalist development will be to generate a less rather than a more revolutionary proletariat.

But once again the coin has two sides. If imperialist exploitation brings wealth to the industrialized countries and enables them to raise further the standard of living of their working classes, it brings poverty and misery to the great mass of the working people—agricultural as well as industrial—in the dependencies. These masses now become an agent of revolutionary change in precisely the sense that Marx believed the industrial proletariat of the mid-nineteenth century to be. Let me quote again what he wrote in the *Holy Family:*

> Because the abstraction of all humanity, even the appearance of humanity, is practically complete in the fully developed proletariat, because the living conditions of the proletariat represent the focal point of all inhuman conditions in contemporary society, because the human being is lost in the proletariat, but has won a theoretical consciousness of loss and is compelled by unavoidable and absolutely compulsory need . . . to revolt against this inhumanity—all these are the reasons why the proletariat can and must emancipate itself.[6]

These words certainly do not apply to the working classes of the United States and Western Europe today. But do they not apply all the more obviously and forcefully to the masses in the much more numerous and populous underdeveloped dependencies of the global capitalist system? And does not the pattern of successful socialist revolutions since the Second World War—highlighted by Vietnam, China, and Cuba—demonstrate beyond any doubt that these masses do indeed constitute a revolutionary agent capable of challenging and defeating capitalism?

Allow me in conclusion to present a very brief summary of my thesis: In Marx's theory of capitalism, the proletariat is not always and necessarily revolutionary. It was not revolutionary in the period of manufacture, becoming so only as a consequence of the introduction of machinery in the industrial revolution. The long-run effects of machinery, however, are different from the immediate effects. If the revolutionary opportunities of the early period of modern industry are missed, the proletariat of an industrializing country tends to become less and less revolutionary. This does not mean, however, that Marx's contention that capitalism produces its own gravediggers is wrong. If we consider capitalism as a global system, which is the only correct procedure, we see that it is divided into a handful of exploiting countries and a much more numerous and populous group of exploited countries. The masses in these exploited dependencies constitute a force in the global capitalist system which is revolutionary in the same sense and for the same reasons that Marx considered the proletariat of the early period of modern industry to be revolutionary. And finally, world history since the Second World War proves that this revolutionary force is really capable of waging successful revolutionary struggles against capitalist domination.

Notes:

1. Karl Marx and Friedrich Engels, *Werke,* vol. 2, p. 38. Except for the first two sentences, the translation is that of the English edition of Mehring, *Karl Marx,* pp. 130-31.
2. *Capital,* I, p. 18. (All page references in the text below are to *Capital,* I.)
3. Nathan Rosenberg, "Adam Smith on the Division of Labour: Two Views or One?" *Economica,* XXXII (May 1965).
4. As a matter of fact, Marx's treatment of the relations among industry, technology, and science was far ahead of his time and has only become fully realistic and applicable a hundred years later.
5. James Boggs, *The American Revolution* (New York: Monthly Review Press, 1963), p. 14.
6. Marx and Engels, *Werke,* vol. 2, p. 38.

Notes on the Centennial
of *Das Kapital*

One hundred years ago—to be exact, in September 1867—the first volume of Karl Marx's *Das Kapital* was published in Hamburg, Germany. The event marked a turning point not only in the history of political economy but in the entire scientific-intellectual development of the modern world. The very embodiment of materialist dialectics, *Das Kapital* presented an indictment of the present and a vision of the future of unprecedented power and passion. Those who recognized in it a revelation of truth—and their number has never ceased to increase—became disciples and followers. The others, much as they might want to, could not ignore it. Many were profoundly influenced, often without their knowledge and sometimes even against their will. And the opponents, for whom it was strictly from the devil, had to fight it as best they could. After a hundred years, Karl Marx and his magnum opus occupy a position in the intellectual life of humanity which is without precedent and without comparison.

This article appeared in the December 1967 issue of *Monthly Review*.

It is not to this grand theme that we propose to address ourselves in these notes, however, but to certain issues in political economy which a century after the publication of *Das Kapital* seem in need of clarification or further study.[1]

Marx and the Classics

It is a commonplace that Marx learned political economy from the English classical school, and particularly from its greatest figure, David Ricardo. In many ways, indeed, Marx's work is a logical continuation and development of classical theory. This holds above all for his conceptual apparatus— value, surplus value, organic composition of capital, rate of profit, etc.—most of which was present, at least in embryonic form, in Ricardo. And yet the conclusions reached in Marx's *Kapital* are miles apart from those of Ricardo's *Principles.*

Both Ricardo and Marx saw the driving force of capitalist development in the accumulation process. But what Ricardo derived was a sort of law of economic entropy, ending in the famous "stationary state." Accumulation involved hiring more workers and cultivating progressively less fertile land, thus raising the rent of all previously cultivated land. Since (in the classical view) wages were fixed at the lowest level compatible with the required expansion of the population, the increasing take of the landlords could only be at the expense of the capitalist's profit. The logical end of this process would come when profit had been squeezed down to the point where the capitalist lacked either the ability or the motivation to go on accumulating. Economic progress would thus be brought to a halt by what the classics regarded as two overriding natural laws: the law of diminishing returns and the Malthusian law of population. It was this vision which caused Carlyle to brand political economy the "dismal science."

Marx's view of the accumulation process and its outcome was of course entirely different. The capitalists protect their profits by introducing ever more and better machinery which both raises the productivity of labor and throws workers out of jobs and into the "industrial reserve army." It is the latter, which Marx also called "relative surplus population," and not Malthusian population pressure which keeps wages in line. In this analysis of the accumulation process, the old bogeys of the classics—diminishing returns and Malthusianism—simply disappear. In their place, however, Marx discovered a whole series of contradictions, unsuspected by his predecessors, which pointed to an entirely different future for the capitalist system. In the first place, there were all the forces making for economic cycles and crises: anarchy of capitalist production, falling tendency of the rate of profit, growing disproportionality between capacity to produce and capacity to consume. Secondly, there was the process which Marx called the concentration and centralization of capital, involving the "expropriation of many capitalists by few." And finally, there was the growth of an increasingly exploited, disciplined, and potentially revolutionary proletariat.[2] All of these forces and tendencies, combining and interacting, were leading to an inevitable climax:

> The monopoly of capital becomes a fetter upon the mode of production, which has sprung up and flourished along with, and under it. Centralization of the means of production and socialization of labor at last reach a point where they become incompatible with their capitalist integument. This integument is burst asunder. The knell of capitalist private property sounds. The expropriators are expropriated. [P. 837]

How are we to account for the fact that Marx, using a conceptual apparatus derived from and similar to that of the classics, nevertheless reached such radically different conclusions? One is tempted to answer that the explanation lies in the different class interests espoused by Marx. A moment's reflection, however, will show that this is not so. Classical political economy, especially in its most developed Ricardian form, was entirely compatible with a theory of class struggle. Indeed, it highlighted the conflict of interests between capitalists and landlords, and the so-called Ricardian socialists soon showed that the theory was equally capable of explaining a conflict of interests between capitalists and workers. Like these anticapitalist writers—with whose work he was of course familiar—Marx could have championed the cause of the working class without making any important changes in classical economic theory. That he did not do so but instead transformed classical political economy into a radically new theory of economic and social development must be explained by something other than class interest and allegiance.

The most satisfactory explanation seems to be that real and fundamental changes took place in the capitalist system between the period when classical political economy took shape in the eighteenth century and the period when Marx wrote *Das Kapital* approximately a hundred years later.[3] These changes were effected by what Marx was one of the first to call the industrial revolution, which took place precisely during these hundred years. The capitalism of the middle of the eighteenth century was dominated on the industrial side by what Marx called the system of manufacture. Here the methods and instruments of production were essentially those of the artisan workshop, but the gathering of many workers under a single roof made possible the kind of elaborate division of labor which Adam Smith so admired and praised as the true secret of increasing productivity and wealth. To the system which emerged from the industrial revolution Marx gave the name of modern industry. Its hallmark was production by machinery, first introduced on a large scale in the textile industry in the eighteenth century and gradually spreading to other key industries. The final step was to "construct machines by machines."

> It was not till it [modern industry] did this that it built up for itself a fitting technical foundation, and stood on its own feet. Machinery, simultaneously with the increasing use of it, in the first decades of this century, appropriated, by degrees, the fabrication of machines proper. But it was only during the decade preceding 1866 that the construction of railways and ocean steamers on a stupendous scale called into existence the cyclopean machines now employed in the construction of prime movers. [P. 420]

The replacement of manufacture by machinery necessarily meant the transformation of capitalism's laws of motion. For, as Marx wrote:

> Modern industry never looks upon and treats the existing form of a process as final. *The technical basis of that industry is therefore revolutionary, while all earlier modes of production were essentially conservative.* By means of machinery, chemical processes, and other methods, it is continually causing changes not only in the technical basis of production, but also in the functions of the laborer and in the labor-process. [Pp. 532-33; emphasis added] [4]

Since classical political economy dealt with one of these earlier "essentially conservative" modes of production, it is not surprising that it envisaged a development process characterized by purely quantitative changes ending in a state of rest (the stationary state). However, the categories of classical political economy were derived from the class structure of capitalism and not from the mode of production of the period of manufacture. They could therefore be taken over, perfected, and used by Marx to analyze the *modus operandi* of capitalism in the period of modern industry.

The classics could afford an objective analysis of the capitalism of their day because, apart from the transforming action of the industrial revolution which could only be understood later, it was in truth not a crisis-laden system headed for explosions and disasters. By the middle of the nineteenth century this was no longer so. The industrial revolution had done its work, and the machinery-based system of modern industry was irrevocably launched on the course which led to the great wars and revolutions of the twentieth century. Bourgeois political economy could not honestly face this situation, and it therefore rapidly degenerated, first producing what Marx called a "herd of vulgar economic apologists" (p. 669n) and then, with the ascendance of the various marginal utility schools, retreating altogether from the realities of the capitalist system. It was left for Marx and his followers to carry on in the honorable scientific tradition which classical political economy had pioneered.

Development in the Advanced Countries

Except for the next-to-last chapter entitled "The So-called Primitive Accumulation,"[5] *Das Kapital* is concerned with the analysis of a capitalist society in which modern industry has already achieved dominance and the accumulation of capital takes place through the investment of capitalistically produced surplus value. Contemporary Britain of course provided most of the empirical material from which Marx distilled his generalizations. And it was obvious that it was in such a country or group of countries that he expected the process of capitalist development to run its course and produce its own negation in the shape of the socialist revolution. It is true that during the last years of his life, Marx—and Engels after Marx's death—began to think in terms of the next wave of revolutions starting in Tsarist Russia; but this did not lead to any changes in theoretical position, and both men continued to believe that the decisive struggles would be fought out in the advanced capitalist countries.

Given this background and given the fact that for the first half century after the publication of Volume I revolutionary movements grew to importance only in Europe and North America, it was only to be expected that political economists among Marx's followers would continue to concentrate their attention on the development of capitalism in the advanced countries. Much discussion and debate took place on such subjects as the nature of economic fluctuations and crises; whether crises are getting more or less severe; whether capitalism is headed for a specifically economic collapse; the economic and social consequences of the concentration and centralization of capital; the emergence and consequences of finance capital; the economic role of the state; and the driving force behind the imperialist expansion of the great capitalist powers.

It is obviously impossible in a brief essay to review the extensive literature dealing with these subjects or to attempt to relate the various positions taken by the protagonists to Marx's theory as set forth in *Das Kapital*.[6] What we want to emphasize is that for the most part these controversies shared a common point of departure which was unquestionably derived from Marx himself: they all took for granted that the arena of decision for the future of capitalism (and socialism) would be the advanced countries of Europe and North America. Even those who appreciated the enormous revolutionary potential of Russia—and their number included, even before the abortive revolution of 1905, such outstanding figures as Kautsky, Rosa Luxemburg, and Lenin—thought of that country primarily as the potential initiator of a general European revolution. It did not occur to them that the main impact of a successful Russian revolution would be, not on the advanced countries of the West but on their much more numerous and vastly more populous colonies and dependencies in what is nowadays called the Third World. It was not until *after* the revolution of 1917, and only in the light of actual historical developments, that Marxists began to understand that the world revolution was taking a course very different from the one they had expected. Even then they were slow to grasp the full significance of this fact and to provide an adequate theoretical explanation. And to this day they have not faced squarely up to the question whether the history of the world revolution during the last half century is or is not compatible with the fundamental theoretical schema of *Das Kapital*. It is to these questions that we now turn.

Development of the Dependent Countries

In the preface to the French and German editions of *Imperialism, the Highest Stage of Capitalism,* Lenin wrote: "Capitalism has grown into a world system of colonial oppression and of the financial strangulation of the overwhelming majority of the people of the world by a handful of 'advanced' countries." *Imperialism* was not, however, an attempt to analyze the functioning of this "world system" considered as a whole. Its purpose was the more limited and urgent one of explaining the nature of the war then raging—the work was written in 1916—and what revolutionaries in the warring countries should do about it. This required that Lenin focus attention on the "handful of 'advanced' countries" (which were doing the fighting) and take into account the "overwhelming majority of the people of the world" only to the extent that they were the objects of the policies of their oppressors and strangulators. Like most other Marxists at the time, Lenin believed that an end would be put to this monstrous system by proletarian revolutions in Europe. And when the Russian Revolution triumphed in 1917, he, again like other Marxists, regarded it as but the prelude to a revolution at least in Germany and possibly in all of Central and Western Europe. How confident he was in the correctness of this prognosis is well reflected in the last two paragraphs of his famous polemic against Kautsky, *The Proletarian Revolution and the Renegade Kautsky,* dated November 10, 1918:

> The above lines were written on November 9, 1918. That same night news was received from Germany announcing the beginning of a victorious revolution, first in Kiel and other northern towns and ports, where the power has passed into the hands of Soviets of Workers' and Soldiers' Deputies, then in Berlin, where, too, power has passed into the hands of a Soviet.
>
> The conclusion which still remained to be written to my pamphlet on Kautsky and on the proletarian revolution is now superfluous.

Appearances, unfortunately, were deceiving. The 1918 revolution in Germany remained at the purely political level, leaving the capitalist order itself intact; and later revolutions in the aftermath of the war were either similar (Austria) or were suppressed (Hungary and Bavaria). It is probably safe to say that most Marxists at the time did not understand the significance of these defeats, believing them to be merely temporary setbacks to be followed in due course by a new, and this time victorious, revolutionary wave in the developed capitalist countries of Europe.

History took a different course. After the failure of the postwar revolutions, Europe ceased to be the center of international revolutionary movements. From that time on, revolutionary initiative shifted away from what Lenin had called the handful of advanced countries to their victims, the overwhelming majority of the people of the world. And it was a measure of Lenin's genius that in the very few years remaining before his death he saw this shift coming and sensed its epoch-making significance. In the last thing he ever wrote for publication, "Better Fewer, But Better," which appeared in *Pravda* on March 2, 1923, Lenin said:

> The system of international relationships which has now taken shape is a system in which one of the states of Europe, viz., Germany, has been enslaved by the victor countries. Furthermore, a number of states, namely, the oldest states in the West, are in a position to utilize their victory to make a number of insignificant concessions to their oppressed classes—concessions which, insignificant though they are, nevertheless retard the revolutionary movement in those countries and create some semblance of "social peace."
>
> At the same time, precisely as a result of the last imperialist war, a number of countries—the East, India, China, etc.—have been completely dislodged from their groove. Their development has definitely shifted to the European capitalist lines. The general European ferment has begun to affect them, and it is now clear to the whole world that they have been drawn into a process of development that cannot but lead to a crisis in the whole of world capitalism.
>
> Thus at the present time we are confronted with the question: Shall we be able to hold on with our small and very small peasant production, and in our present state of ruin, while the West-European capitalist countries are consummating their development toward socialism? But they are consummating it not as we formerly expected. They are not consummating it by the gradual "maturing" of socialism, but by the exploitation of some countries by others, by the exploitation of the first of the countries to be vanquished in the imperialist war combined with the exploitation of the whole of the East. On the other hand, precisely as a result of the first imperialist war, the East has been definitely drawn into the revolutionary movement, has been definitely drawn into the general maelstrom of the world revolutionary movement. . . .

In the last analysis, the outcome of the struggle will be determined by the fact that Russia, India, China, etc., account for the overwhelming majority of the population of the globe. And it is precisely this majority that, during the past few years, has been drawn into the struggle for emancipation with extraordinary rapidity, so that in this respect there cannot be the slightest shadow of doubt what the final outcome of the world struggle will be. In this sense, the complete victory of socialism is fully and absolutely assured.

It is true that at several points in this exposition Lenin's meaning is not altogether clear. In particular, the idea that the European capitalist countries "are consummating their advance toward socialism . . . by the exploitation of some countries by others" can be interpreted in different ways. Nevertheless there can be no doubt at all that Lenin had abandoned the traditional Marxist view that the socialist revolution was essentially an affair of the advanced countries and that the fate of the rest of the world depended on the success or failure of their proletariats. The scene had definitely and irrevocably shifted to the whole globe, and there was at least the possibility that thenceforth the main actors would be the underdeveloped countries.

With the development of revolutionary and national independence struggles in the Third World—especially in China and India, the world's two most populous countries— this global view of the revolutionary process came to be increasingly accepted among Marxists. And it should logically have led to a systematic, scientific study and analysis of a whole series of problems which Marxist theory, because of its preoccupation with the development of the advanced countries, had hitherto ignored or treated only incidentally. What needed investigating above all was the typical course of development of a country which entered the capitalist system as the colony or dependency of an advanced country—typical in the same sense that *Das Kapital* had investigated the typical course of development of a capitalist country which had already been through the historical experiences of primitive accumulation and industrial revolution.

One may speculate that if Lenin had lived, such work might have been undertaken and the international Communist movement might have been provided with crucially important understanding of the functioning of capitalism not just as a system existing in the industrialized West but as a global system of exploiting and exploited nations. Unfortunately Lenin did not live and the work was not undertaken. What happened instead was a more or less mechanical application to the new situation of theories familiar to all Marxists since the publication of the *Communist Manifesto*. Capitalism in Europe had emerged out of feudalism and had consolidated its power through a bourgeois revolution, i.e., a revolution led by the bourgeoisie in alliance with workers and peasants. After that—in some cases, as in Russia in 1917, very soon after that—would come the proletarian revolution and the beginning of the transition from capitalism to socialism.

This schema was now applied to the colonies and dependencies containing the great majority of the world's population. The prevailing state of backwardness was equated with European feudalism and local bourgeoisies with the rising mercantile and industrial capitalists of the West. To maintain its power, imperialism had allied itself with the feudalists. In this situation it was assumed that the colonial bourgeoisies would take the lead in fighting against both feudalism and imperialism, and that it was the duty of revolutionaries representing the interests of the masses to support them in this two-sided struggle. Victory would be followed by national independence, bourgeois-democratic reforms, and the opening of a new struggle for the proletarian-socialist revolution.

Wherever this theory was acted upon, the result was failure and in some cases disaster. China in the mid-1920s is the most striking example. Chiang Kai-shek and the Kuomintang, supposedly representing a national bourgeoisie in the fight against feudalism and for independence, proved in practice to be agents and allies of imperialism who turned against their Communist supporters and slaughtered them wholesale. But it was not only as a guide to action that the theory fell down. The expectations to which it gave rise were nowhere realized, and its explanatory value has been consistently negative.

Challenges to this new brand of Marxist orthodoxy gradually developed from two entirely different quarters. After its defeats of 1927 the Chinese Communist Party under Mao Tse-tung's leadership re-formed in the countryside and hammered out a new revolutionary conception which relegated the national bourgeoisie to a mere followership role and recognized that serious reform, whether of a bourgeois-democratic or socialist nature, would be possible only after the seizure of power by the party of the workers and peasants. While this political line was being developed in practice in China, some Marxists in the West were working toward a more adequate theory of capitalism-imperialism considered as a global system, with special emphasis on the nature and effects of imperialist economic relations on the underdeveloped colonies and dependencies.

The history of this intellectual development will have to be written some day: here we will be content to mention two important milestones, R. Palme Dutt's *India Today* and Paul A. Baran's *Political Economy of Growth*.[7] Dutt's book is a brilliant, fully documented study of the economic (and social) ruination of India under British rule. Its most serious flaw is that the author, under the influence of the Communist orthodoxy of the twenties and thirties, still imagined that the Indian bourgeoisie, even though the product of a long degenerative process, could play a progressive historical role. A reader of the book when it appeared could never again be unaware of the devastating impact of imperialism on its victims, but he would not have been prepared for the tragedy of independent India ruled by its own bourgeoisie. Baran's book was perhaps the first to put forward a general theory of the dialectical interrelation of development in the industrialized countries and underdevelopment in the colonies and dependencies, and as such it made a tremendous impression on many younger Marxists, especially in the Third World.[8]

What all this adds up to is that the whole complex of policies and ideas which rested on the assumption of an essential similarity between the transition from feudalism to capitalism in Western Europe on the one hand and the national liberation of capitalism's colonies and dependencies on the other—this whole complex has been decisively refuted both practically and theoretically. It is too early to say that in its place an adequate theory of world capitalism and the means necessary to overthrow it has been worked out. But much progress has been made, and there is every reason to hope that the goal will be reached in the not distant future.

Marx's Position

Marx opened the Preface to the *Critique of Political Economy* (1859) with the following sentence: "I consider the system of bourgeois economy in the following order: *Capital, landed property, wage labor; state, foreign trade, world market.*" By the time he wrote the first volume of *Das Kapital* he had already abandoned this outline, and he never returned to it. As a result we have no systematic exposition from his pen of the last three topics—state, foreign trade, world market. This is too bad, because if Marx had written specifically and at length on these subjects, the chances are good that he would have established a framework of thinking about capitalism as an international, worldwide system which might have served his followers well when the course of history obliged them to adopt precisely such a perspective. As it is, all we can do is attempt to show that he did have a position and that as far as it goes it foreshadows, and is fully compatible with, the best modern work in this area.

There are two parts of Volume I which are particularly relevant: (a) the section of the chapter on primitive accumulation entitled "Genesis of the Industrial Capitalist" (pp. 822-34 in the English edition); and (b) a passage from the chapter on machinery and modern industry (pp. 492-93; this passage is cited below, p. 182). The first deals with the early impact of the emerging capitalist countries on the rest of the world, the second with the consequences of machinery and modern industry for relations between the developed and underdeveloped countries.

(1) *The Early Impact.* Under this heading we need do no more, and could do no better, than quote several passages dispersed through the chapter in question:

> The discovery of gold and silver in America, the extirpation, enslavement, and entombment in mines of the aboriginal population, the beginning of the conquest and looting of the East Indies, the turning of Africa into a warren for the commercial hunting of black-skins, signalized the rosy dawn of the era of capitalist production. [P. 823]

> To secure Malacca, the Dutch corrupted the Portuguese governor. He let them into the town in 1641. They hurried at once to his house and assassinated him, to "abstain" from the payment of £21,875, the price of his treason. Wherever they set foot, devastation and depopulation followed. Banjuwangi, a province of Java, in 1750 numbered over 80,000 inhabitants, in 1811 only 18,000. Sweet commerce! [P. 824]

The treatment of the aborigines was, naturally, most frightful in plantation-colonies destined for export trade only, such as the West Indies, and in rich and well-populated countries, such as Mexico and India, that were given over to plunder. [P. 825]

The colonial system ripened, like a hot house, trade and navigation. . . . The colonies secured a market for the budding manufacturers, and, through the monopoly of the market, an increased accumulation. The treasures captured outside Europe by undisguised looting, enslavement, and murder, floated back to the mother country and were there turned into capital. [P. 826]

The system of protection was an artificial means of manufacturing manufacturers, of expropriating independent laborers, of capitalizing the national means of production and subsistence, of forcibly abbreviating the transition from the medieval to the modern mode of production. The European states tore each other to pieces about the patent of this invention, and, once entered into the service of the surplus-value makers, did not merely lay under contribution in the pursuit of this purpose their own people, indirectly through protective duties, directly through export premiums. They also forcibly rooted out, in their dependent countries, all industry. . . . [P. 830]

Whilst the cotton industry introduced child slavery in England, it gave in the United States a stimulus to the transformation of the earlier, more or less patriarchal slavery, into a system of commercial exploitation. In fact, the veiled slavery of the wage earners in Europe needed, for its pedestal, slavery pure and simple in the new world. [P. 833]

(2) *Machinery and Modern Industry.* As the above quotations indicate, capitalism in Europe came into existence not only through looting the rest of the world of its accumulated

treasures but also through actively ruining their established social systems. Did a more productive and "civilized" capitalism later make amends? Here is Marx's answer:

> On the one hand, the immediate effect of machinery is to increase the supply of raw material in the same way, for example, as the cotton gin augmented the production of cotton. On the other hand, the cheapness of the articles produced by machinery, and the improved means of transport and communication furnish the weapons for conquering foreign markets. By ruining handicraft production in other countries, machinery forcibly converts them into fields for the supply of its raw material. In this way East India was compelled to produce cotton, wool, hemp, jute, and indigo for Great Britain. By constantly making a part of the hands "supernumerary," modern industry, in all countries where it has taken root, gives a spur to emigration and to the colonization of foreign lands, which are thereby converted into settlements for growing the raw material of the mother country. . . . A new and international division of labor, a division suited to the requirements of the chief centers of modern industry springs up and converts one part of the globe into a chiefly agricultural field of production, for supplying the other part which remains a chiefly industrial field. [Pp. 492-93]

The impact of capitalism on the rest of the world was thus by no means confined to its early stages but continued into the period of modern industry—with this difference, that now its weapons were less the open, brutal use of force and more the insidious penetrating power of the market. If one looked at capitalism as a global system, the progress of the advanced sector was at all stages the direct cause of retrogression in the remainder. Long before he wrote *Das Kapital,* Marx had observed and commented upon this process at work in the relationship between Britain and India:

There cannot . . . remain any doubt but that the misery inflicted by the British on Hindustan is of an essentially different and infinitely more intensive kind than all Hindustan had to suffer before. . . .

All the civil wars, invasions, revolutions, conquests, famines, strangely complex, rapid and destructive as the successive action in Hindustan may appear, did not go deeper than its surface. England has broken down the entire framework of Indian society, without any symptoms of reconstitution yet appearing. This loss of his old world, with no gain of a new one, imparts a particular kind of melancholy to the present misery of the Hindu, and separates Hindustan, ruled by Britain, from all its ancient traditions, and from the whole of its past history.[9]

There is thus no doubt that Marx was fully aware of the causal relationship between the development of capitalism in Europe and the development of underdevelopment in the rest of the world. He had the basic elements of a theory of capitalism as a global system, and the pity is that his followers did not see this in good time and understand the importance of extending and developing his ideas. If they had, they surely could not have believed that the colonies and dependencies of the capitalist empires were in a state of "feudalism" or that their crippled and dependent economies could produce other than a crippled and dependent bourgeoisie. They would thus have seen from the outset the absurdity of treating the theoretical schema of the *Communist Manifesto* as a universal formula.

In reality these lessons had to be learned a harder way, and unfortunately there are many who consider themselves Marxists who have still not learned them. For them, the centennial of *Das Kapital* could well be an occasion to read, or re-read, the works of the master and to seek earnestly to bring their thinking into line with his.

Notes:

1. We continue to use the German title because it was not until twenty years later, in 1887, that an English translation of Volume I was published. In this connection it is interesting to note that the first foreign translation was the Russian, which appeared in 1872, fifteen years before the English. In what follows, references are to the Kerr edition of the Moore and Aveling translation.

2. On this and related issues, see "Marx and the Proletariat," pp. 147-65 above.

3. It is true that Ricardo's *Principles* did not appear until 1817. However, he was inspired to write it by reading Adam Smith's *The Wealth of Nations* (1776), and it was Smith's economic reality with which he was concerned. The famous chapter "On Machinery," which raised altogether new problems and in a sense foreshadowed Marx's economic reality, was added as a kind of afterthought to the third edition (1821).

4. Some of the implications of these changes in the "functions of the laborer and in the labor-process" are explored in "Marx and the Proletariat," above. See especially pp. 150-51 ff.

5. In the English translation, this chapter appears as a separate part, and its seven sections as separate chapters.

6. An effort in this direction, with respect to the problems of crises and economic breakdown, is contained in Sweezy, *The Theory of Capitalist Development,* part III, especially chapter 11.

7. R. P. Dutt, *India Today*, 2d. ed. (London: Collet's Ltd., 1950); Paul A. Baran, *The Political Economy of Growth* (New York: Monthly Review Press, 1957).

8. "For me, Paul Baran's systematic examination of the development of underdevelopment as the reverse side of the coin of development under capitalism on a world scale opens the door to the understanding of world history, past, present, and future." The words are those of Andre Gunder Frank, writing in the special Baran memorial issue of *Monthly Review,* March 1965. Frank himself is one of the most important continuators of work in this area.

9. *New York Daily Tribune,* June 25, 1853. Reprinted in Karl Marx and Friedrich Engels, *On Colonialism* (Moscow: no date), pp. 33-34.